D1714232

QUILTING MADE EASY

QUILTING MADE EASY

Mildred Graves Ryan

Drawings by Marta Cone

NELSON DOUBLEDAY, INC.
Garden City, New York

Preface

To many, quilting is the most beautiful and gratifying type of needlework to create. Born of necessity, it has developed into a decorative art that continues to fill a utilitarian need. Work of the past as well as the present has a valued place in the world of needle art. It is sometimes difficult to realize that something that can give such a comfortable, cozy feeling has the possibility of becoming a treasure. But it can, and you have the power to make it so. It just requires the ability to make a simple stitch, to add an artistic touch, and to have the patience and desire to work with precision.

Although there is a certain seriousness to quilting, it is usually done in a happy, relaxed atmosphere. Quilters enjoy watching a needle move in and out of the material. The regularity of the stitches seems to provide a peaceful feeling, allowing time for daydreaming. Royalty and farm folk alike have been involved in the pursuit of quilting.

The versatility of quilting seems limitless. As if by magic, a simple stitch transforms a bit of fabric into something lovely. Variations in shape, color, texture, and technique provide a myriad of looks. There is a difference not only in design but also in the resulting project. Whole-cloth stitching, piecing, appliqué, trapunto, embroidery, and stenciling can each play a part in creating such quilted items as quilts, wall hangings, pillows, tablecloths, place mats, jackets, vests, and accessories. Simple geometric shapes can suddenly be converted into interesting quilted articles.

Because the possibilities are so great, there are many decisions to consider in order for the quilting to give you pleasure and be easy to do. Temperament, skill with a needle, likes and dislikes, space in which to work will influence what you decide to quilt and how you will do it. If you do not have the patience for accuracy, then patchwork will prove troublesome. If finishing something is a priority, do not start a quilt unless you have time and a place to work on it. If you find hand sewing tedious, select designs that can be made by machine. If space is at a premium, work on small projects.

On the following pages you will find information that will help you select a project that is right for you and at the same time easy to make. Different styles are described, traditional designs shown, historical significance traced, techniques explained. Studying all of these factors will provide the background for your quilting.

The material in this book provides the novice with step-by-step descriptions, in words and drawings, of the basic techniques by which the various types of quilting are done and at the same time offers ideas and inspiration to the most accomplished. Frequently one forgets that patchwork is not the only form of quilting. There are many others that create lovely effects. Knowing about them can prove interesting and productive and, in some instances, suggest an easier method.

As you try the various types of quilting, you may become one of those to help quilting further establish its place in the world of fine arts. It can be a fascinating art form, capable of variety and richness, ranging from the elegant to the humorous.

In preparing a book, one needs the assistance and encouragement of friends and associates. For such help, I am especially grateful to Eugenie Rives, Sally Signor, and Sally Wellbery, who allowed me to admire and study their beautiful quilted treasures, and to Loretta Stipe of the McCall Pattern Company, who provided information about the modern aspects of quilted designs. I am also indebted to the museums and organizations and their personnel who provided a wealth of material to be perused.

M.G.R.

Contents

CONTENTS • ix

CONTENTS

QUILTING MADE EASY

1

Quilting—Past and Present

In recent years there has been a resurgence of interest in quilts and quilting. Nicely made old quilts command high prices as they become heirlooms and collectors' items. Decorators find quilting adds excitement to a room. Quilts are thrown over a chair, hung on the wall, or make a casual grouping of patchwork pillows in the most modern of rooms. A quilt may even find its way to a luncheon table or under a Christmas tree.

Designers have made quilting fashionable. It seems everyone, both young and old, has worn a quilted jacket or coat at some time during recent years. The popularity of quilting has been interesting to watch, with new patterns being introduced each year to make the fashion seem new and exciting. Once again, quilting provides warmth and an attractive protectiveness, just as it did when it was introduced centuries ago.

How It Began

Actually the origin of quilting has never really been established. What we do know, however, makes its history sound interesting—romantic at times and at others eminently practical.

Persia, India, and Egypt, where decorative stitching was known as early as the days of Abraham, are possible sites for its birth. Records, though, indicate that quilting was introduced into Europe and the British Isles by the Crusaders as early as

the eleventh and twelfth centuries. The knights had discovered how comfortable it was to follow a Turkish custom of wearing two or three layers of fabric under their armor. The layers were held together by a network of stitches. Sometimes the material was also placed over the armor to protect it from inclement weather.

Because of the warm climate there, the padded material was not used to any extent in Europe until the fourteenth century. Then that area experienced a change in weather patterns: temperatures dropped. The need for warmer clothing and bedding was imperative and quilted material seemed the answer.

THE EARLY DAYS

In the early days of quilting, the fabrics were usually plain and of one color. Interest was centered on the stitches which ran in straight lines and moved in a variety of directions. Later the stitches created more decorative and elaborate designs. Pictures of those designs often show scrolls and sprays circling an ornamental center motif.

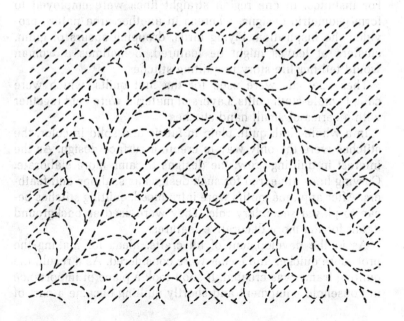

Fabrics became more beautiful as the art progressed. In France and Italy silks and damasks, as well as fine cottons, were employed. Heavier velvets and brocades were preferred by the Spaniards for their work on ecclesiastical vestments.

Sicily seems to have been the place in Italy that specialized in quilting. In fact the oldest known bed quilt was made there in about the year 1400. Because of the climate, a quilt was not necessarily needed for warmth, so more importance was placed on the design and decorative details.

In the fifteenth century a different decorative detail was introduced by the French. Instead of just using sewing and embroidery stitches to create the decoration, they cut the designs out of pieces of material and applied them to other pieces of fabric. This was the beginning of appliqué.

During the fifteenth, sixteenth, and seventeenth centuries quilting was very popular, especially in the Elizabethan period. Gradually the work was refined, developing variations of more complex and artistic stitch patterns. In Great Britain people in certain areas created their own distinctive designs, which you will find still being used today by great-great-granddaughters. For instance, in one region straight lines were employed to form geometric designs, whereas in another area nature provided the inspiration. Flying birds, drooping spears of grain, clusters of leaves might be featured. Sometimes a woman would tell her life story in quilting stitches.

These designs were used for the first quilts, which were called whole-cloth quilts. Layers of material were held together with a series of small hand stitches.

In a whole-cloth quilt, plain in fabric and solid in color, the stitches were the only way to create a surface design. As the interest in quilting grew, the designs became more elaborate. Curving lines appeared for such designs as scallops and feathers. After appliqué motifs were introduced, quilting stitches began to play a secondary role. They were used as background detail for the more decorative features.

As in the development of all crafts, ideas for making the procedure quicker and easier were considered. As a result, the quilting frame was created. It soon took a place of importance in household equipment and shortly quilting became a part of

daily living. The frame was put up in the evening at the completion of the daily chores, the family gathered around, and the needles began to fly as the girls learned to quilt.

Quilt making became so much a part of family life that at an early age a girl started to make quilts for her future home. It was thought that a bride should have twelve quilts plus one, a baker's dozen. Each quilt was different in design, although each one followed the traditional family patterns. A simple top was planned as a beginning project for a little girl. As she grew older the designs became more intricate. Finally, when the day arrived for the announcement of her betrothal, it was time to make the thirteenth quilt, called the bride's quilt, and it was the most beautiful one of all.

IN AMERICA

Just as quilting was reaching the height of its popularity in Europe, people started migrating to the New World. Among their few possessions were their highly prized quilts as well as their quilted petticoats. Although the quilters brought their patterns and favorite designs with them, the demands of the new land brought changes to the routine. The settlers who moved to

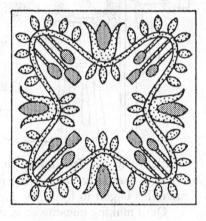

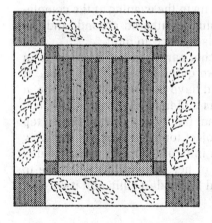

Canada and the northern areas found it easier and quicker to acquire and convert fur into bed coverings than to make quilts. In the South the climate was so mild that quilted bed covering was not needed for warmth. It was therefore left to the immigrants along the middle Atlantic coast to keep the art of quilting alive.

Because the pioneers from different lands settled in separate areas, a distinct difference in quilting designs was established. The Puritans in New England favored sturdy fabrics and simple designs. In New York the Dutch appliquéd their designs to plain material. Quakers, Germans, and Swedes settled in Pennsylvania; probably the most distinctive designs were those of the Germans who were known as Pennsylvania Dutch. The colors were brighter, the designs bolder, and the intricate quilting beautifully done. Glowing reds, yellows, and greens created eye-compelling looks. The colors the Amish used were more subtle but still striking. The tones were grayed and darker, with blue, green, and purple frequently used. The Cavaliers went farther south. Here the appliquéd designs were more delicate and graceful, and interpreted in fine fabrics and pastel colors.

As the years passed, the quilters in New England began to sew small pieces of cloth together to form a larger, decorative piece of fabric instead of just adding patches to old material to prolong its life. This was the beginning of patchwork. As settlers moved westward, this type of needlework began to be called pieced work. Women pieced quilts.

With the advent of the sewing machine and the development of the sewing industry, quilting was no longer an important household activity. Fashions in bed coverings changed and the time-consuming task became more of a pastime. By the latter part of the nineteenth century the interest in quilting had diminished considerably. Today, however, quilting is being done with great enthusiasm and considerable creativity.

Contemporary Quilting

Quilting enters many facets of our lives. To some quilters thinking of themselves as artists it has become an art form. Instead of in canvas and paint, they work in fabric, exploring the fascination of color, texture, and shape. People who appreciate quilting but don't necessarily do it themselves have become collectors and investors, searching for antique quilts, beautifully made and preserved, as others search for masterpieces or soaring stocks that will increase even more in value. Even the theater recognized quilting's potential as a dramatic theme when it presented *The Quilter* on Broadway a few seasons ago. Quilting has been taken from the bed to the wall, from a craft to an art.

The popularity of quilting has grown tremendously during the past fifteen years. Some innovative quilters have tried to express themselves in unusual ways, not only in the materials they use but in the manipulation of them. Brown paper bags, rag paper, Xeroxed chewing gum wrappers, photo-silk screening, galvanized steel wire, and appliquéd shells have appeared. A best-of-show award was given for a framed work made of plastic and color-Xeroxed paper. At such times one wonders when an artistic creation should be listed as a quilt.

Although there has been a great deal of innovation shown by a few, the majority of quilt makers follow traditional footsteps. Old patterns still form the basis for work today. Even though there is a feeling of imitation, there is an attempt to disguise it, giving the quilting an individual touch. A quilter still tries to tell a story or evoke a mood by using traditional geometric shapes and methods. For instance, one quilt artist selected shapes, colors, and textures to conjure up the feeling of cloudiness, wetness, lightning, and sunbeams. Although the design of nine blocks was identical, the colors and textures changed to create the various moods. The greatest satisfaction seems to come when the best of the old blends with the best of the new.

Until one has passed from the category of quilter to that of artist, it seems wise to create a new look in a traditional way through the use of modern colors and textures in interesting

combinations. An artist does not copy a great master but instead tries to profit from his approach to the subject.

Being aware of current trends in other art forms such as films, painting, photography, and weaving proves helpful in developing your ideas. If you have a chance, visit exhibits of antique quilts. Study the patterns and colors. Notice how the impression of movement is created by the juxtaposition of dark and light. Often the placement of the pieces stirs one's imagination. Alternating stripes of orange and dark brown arranged in a Log Cabin pattern may evoke the picture of a furrowed field or of autumn sunshine falling through barn rafters. A willingness to experiment adds a certain individuality to your work.

2

Before You Begin

Quilting offers a chance to show one's artistic ability whether quilting a bedspread, place mats, pillow covers for your home or an eyeglass case, a tote bag, or adding a decorative pocket to a favorite jacket for yourself. For all, an understanding of good design and how it can be produced are required. Lines, shapes, colors, and textures need to be blended into a harmoni-

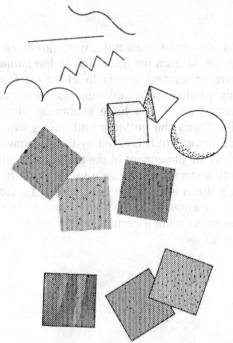

ous whole. It is not enough just to create a beautiful article. The article must seem appropriate for the place it is to be used or the person who will be wearing it. Each line, shape, color, and texture should blend, creating an agreeable unity among the parts. For example, a quilted piece composed of just straight lines may seem uninteresting, but when a curving one is introduced the work takes on a more pleasing look. The same situation may occur when only one color is used. The quilting may have a monotonous, dull appearance. It needs a dash of contrast to make the design interesting, but the amount of contrast should be controlled. Too many elements will produce a discordant effect.

To create the perfect blend isn't as easy as one may think. It requires an eye that is attuned to beauty for both its artistic traits and its practical qualities. This takes practice. Using the elements of design to create various effects is most important. And for the quilter this can be a real pleasure. Experimenting with designs, colors, and fabrics to produce a certain individuality that seems just right can be a fun experience.

Before you begin to plan your quilting design, consider how and where it is to be used. Decide on the look you want to create. Do you want it to be a dominant design feature in a room or just an incidental accent to provide a lively or subdued atmosphere? Have a mental picture of the finished article. Too often one forgets about the total effect when choosing colors and textures for a new item such as a wall hanging or a quilt. One thinks only in terms of the prettiness of the design and not of its appropriateness to its surroundings.

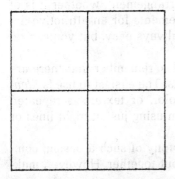
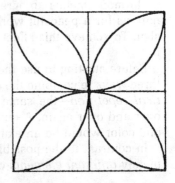

Creating a Design Plan

Sometimes a quilter forgets that the creation of an attractive piece of needlework is an art requiring skill and taste. It is usually impossible to produce a beautiful effect by chance. Just as an artist employs certain guiding rules to achieve a work of art, so too should the quilter. An understanding of the essential elements and principles of design is needed whether the design is a painting, a gown, or a quilt. If rules concern you, don't be upset. These are simply guides to help you select and combine the ingredients of your quilting project so that the finished product will be a perfect display of good design.

To make a brownie, you follow a recipe, so you know exactly what to use and how to combine the ingredients. Although the directions for creating a quilting design aren't quite as specific, you follow the same procedure. Instead of ingredients you use elements of design, and instead of directions, principles to guide you.

If you wonder what elements are, there are five of them—line, shape and space, color, dark and light, and texture. They have to be combined for all designs. In order that the mixing not be done in a haphazard fashion, the principles should be followed. They explain how emphasis, proportion, balance, and rhythm should be used so the effect will be unified and pleasing.

HARMONIOUS EFFECT

Harmony means an agreeable arrangement, whether it is of nations for a peaceful world or elements for an attractive design. To achieve this effect is not always easy, but you can do it.

Before starting to use these guides, remember that there are three ways to combine the elements. The easiest to use is *identical repetition*—the same line, color, or texture is repeated over and over again. A quilt design using just straight lines or one color would be an example.

In contrast to the possible monotony of such a design, completely *different elements* can be put together. However, mak-

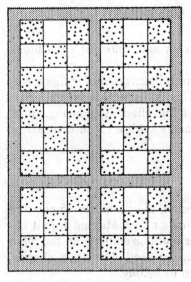

Identical Repetition

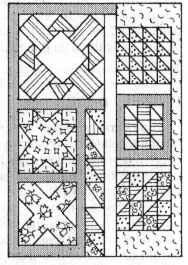

Different Elements

Similar Lines, Colors & Textures

ing a quilt using a different design and color for each block would create confusion.

In order to avoid monotony and discord, *similar lines, colors, and textures* can be used. This is the way to create a harmonious effect. To be sure that the effect is pleasing, there should be unity among the elements with a bit of contrast or variety.

UNITY IN DESIGN

To produce *coherence* in a design, the parts should seem to belong together, resulting in a single effect. Making a quilt because it is pretty isn't enough. It should be suitable for the room and furnishings in which it is to be used. The lines, shapes, colors, and textures should seem to belong.

Also to create unity, it is necessary to emphasize one type of line, shape, color, or texture more than another. For example, if both dark and light hues are to be employed in a design, there should be more of one than of another. The same procedure should be followed when selecting lines and textures, such as more straight than curved, dull than shiny.

There should also be a perfect blending of the colors as well as of the tints and shades. Perhaps you have seen a wall hanging in which one color seemed to jump out of the design and hit you in the eye. Of course it destroyed the sense of unity. Although one color and one value should dominate the design, they should be blended nicely.

Textures should follow this related pattern. They should be suitable for one another as well as to the quilting's final use. You shouldn't attempt to make a patchwork square of organdy and percale, or use a delicate print in a rugged cabin.

DOMINANT NOTE

A center of interest or focal point with other details subordinated to it is needed for a good design. Use the principle of emphasis to create interest in the design by attracting the eye to one part. If you study a painting by a great artist, you can see how it has been done. In planning a quilting design, you

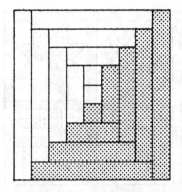 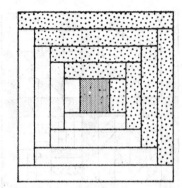

should think of it not only as part of your room decoration but also as a work of art.

Calling attention to one area can be done in several ways. A difference in line, shape, color, and texture, such as a bright square for the center of a Log Cabin design when the other pieces are rectangular in shape and subdued in color produces a center of interest.

Another way to create a dominant note is by using the unusual in line, shape, and color. For example, one block with an embroidered signature will capture the eye when the other blocks are without this distinctive addition.

RIGHT PROPORTION

Since one part of the design should be emphasized, you should learn how to subordinate lesser details to the more important. Here the principle of proportion will help you solve the problem.

Proportion controls the association of one part of a design to another. For example, when a quilt designer creates a new design, she thinks about the size of each part: the size of the block, the width of the setting strips, the border, and of course the design detail in relation to the size of the quilt itself. If the details are too small or too large, or if she fails to subordinate the less important features to the more significant ones, the resulting design will be unattractive. See next page.

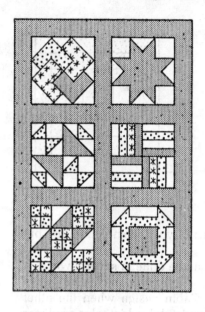 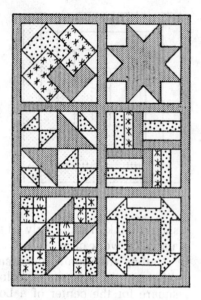

Although the problem of good proportion has been solved by mathematicians, the question of dividing a quilting design into attractive parts should be thought of as something more than a mathematical problem. To develop a feeling for good proportion, you should know that it is based on unequal divisions that fall somewhere between one half and two thirds of an area.

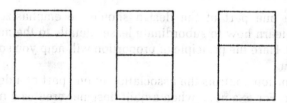

You should also realize that very unequal sizes and amounts will seem as bad as those of equal proportions. This is one of

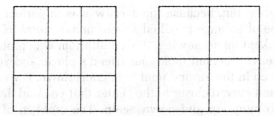

the reasons why a nine-patch design seems more interesting than one of four patches. If you are quilting a jacket, then its length should be thought of in connection with the length of your skirt and the height of your figure. Notice how variations in the length of a coat affect the appearance of one's figure.

RESTFUL BALANCE

No doubt you learned about balance at an early age. Remember your first experience on a seesaw? Perhaps a friend who was the same weight rode with you. You went up and down, having great fun, because the seesaw was in perfect balance. This type of balance is called *formal* or *symmetrical*.

If you kept on seesawing, this equilibrium was probably upset. A heavier person took your friend's place, and you found yourself up in the air and unable to come down. It wasn't until this person moved closer to the center that you and the seesaw began to move up and down again. The problem of balance was solved. This type of balance is called *informal* or *asymmetrical*.

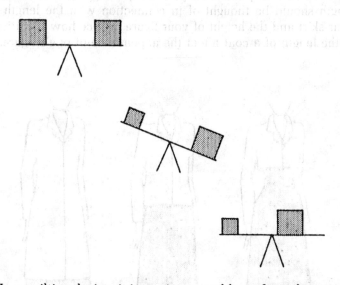

In a quilting design, it is not just a problem of weights as it is with the seesaw. Instead it is a balance of the elements of design—lines, space, colors, values, and textures—depending on their power of attraction or apparent weight. For example, the same amounts of bright and dull colors do not have the same power of attraction. Learning how to arrange the elements so that the design will appear poised and restful is most important.

When the elements are the same or appear so on each side of the imaginary center, formal balance is produced, a balance that is simple and poised. Blocks with identical designs placed on each side of the center and the same distance from it achieve this type of balance.

Informal balance is more difficult to create. Placing unlike elements on either side of the center so that the completed design has a feeling of equilibrium takes practice. No doubt you have seen a quilt that seemed lopsided because the blocks on one side seemed more prominent than those on the other.

It is also important to consider the design on a horizontal plane as well as on a vertical one. Equal divisions are pleasing on a vertical plane. However, there is a possibility that an object will appear top-heavy if it is divided into equal parts on the horizontal plane. This is especially important to remember when quilting a jacket for yourself. It will be better if the imaginary center is placed so that the upper part is slightly smaller than the lower part.

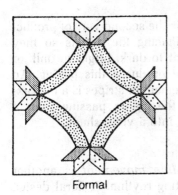

Formal

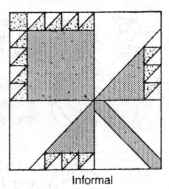

Informal

DEVELOPING RHYTHM

Developing rhythm in a design is often compared to dancing. Some people seem to glide in a smooth, graceful fashion, others to bounce and jerk in an awkward motion. For a design to appear attractive, the eye must move in a flowing motion from one part to another. If the eye jumps back and forth in a helter-skelter fashion, the opposite is true. The design looks unattractive.

Keeping the eye moving in an orderly fashion can be done in several ways. Repetition, gradation, and unbroken line direction produce this rhythmic effect. The significant factor to remember is that the eye must be led on and on from one detail to another. It must never be allowed to actually stop and study a detail, but instead just to quickly pause and then be drawn on to a more interesting feature. To do this, each detail should be placed so that the eye moves easily from one detail to another.

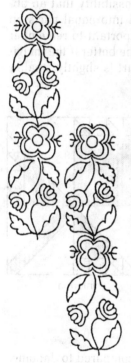

Repetition is probably the easiest way to obtain rhythm in a design. A series of stripes the same width placed carefully will carry the eye in the direction desired.

Gradation is the second way of producing rhythm. Placing the details so they flow from light to dark, bright to dull, or small to large produces this feeling. An ombré arrangement of stripes is a nice example, with the colors passing from a very pale tint into a vivid shade.

Unbroken line movement is another way for creating rhythm. A floral design with undulating stems can produce this effect.

GOOD LINE

Lines combine to shape a design and fill it with details. Some of these lines are straight, others curved. Some follow a vertical direction, others a horizontal or a diagonal one.

Straight or Curved. Straight lines are direct. They carry the eye firmly in one direction. Short straight lines, however, and little zigzag lines may appear sprightly and at the same time give a somewhat nervous feeling. You can see that effect in some of the pieced work.

Curved lines, when they are restrained, are usually considered more graceful than straight lines. Again they carry the eye in a specific direction, but in a more relaxed way. Curved lines should be modified and controlled for greatest interest.

The direction a line takes is most important in setting the mood of a design. A vertical-line direction gives a feeling of dignity and sophistication, whereas a horizontal one creates a restful, gentle feeling. Diagonal lines combine the two, modifying either mood. For the greatest interest, vary the lines and shapes you use.

COLOR INTEREST

Although there wouldn't be a design without line, the importance of color should not be ignored. The world would be a very gloomy place without it. Even though we are surrounded by lovely natural color schemes, it often seems very difficult for the average person to arrange colors wisely and well. Frequently color is used with such abundance that the effect seems loud and intrusive. Instead, color should be used skillfully so the design is alive and arresting, but with a subtlety that seems a part of good taste.

In order to employ color correctly, you should understand how it is formed. Dissecting a color into its parts is important. You should be able to see the hue or hues it contains, the value and intensity. You will then find it easier to choose and combine the various hues.

Color Traits. The number of colors we see every day seems tremendous. Yet they can all be tracked to three colors—red, yellow, and blue. These are called the primary colors. Combining two of them in equal amounts creates another group of

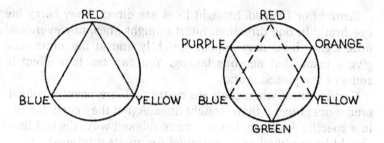

colors called secondaries—orange, green, and purple. From this point, you can proceed on and on, creating a limitless number of variations.

Other changes are formed by a variation in *intensity* (brightness or dullness) and in *value* (lightness and darkness). When white is added to a hue, a tint is produced; with black, a shade. This makes it possible to have light and dark colors.

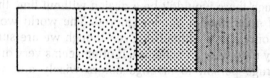

Illusions can also be created by colors. Tints make an object seem larger; shades, smaller. For example, a bed covered in pale blue will seem bigger than one covered in dark blue.

COLORS IN COMBINATION

A *color harmony* or scheme is a combination of tints and shades of a color or a combination of different hues that blend to produce an effect. The simplest of these combinations is a *monochromatic scheme,* produced by using tints and shades of the same hue. One of the most interesting of these is a blending of orange with its tint (beige) and shade (brown).

Colors that are next to each other on the color wheel can be joined to create an *analogous* or *related color scheme*. Blue combined with green would be an example of this type of harmony.

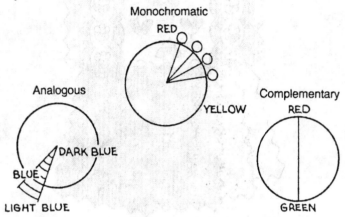

A *complementary color harmony* uses hues that are opposite each other on the color wheel. For example, combinations of red and green, yellow and purple, blue and orange fall into this color pattern.

Using white and black, which are neutral colors, with a hue such as red can be interesting. This type of color harmony is known as an *accented neutral.*

Even though you can create a color scheme by working with a color wheel, it is also possible to develop one from a scheme that has already been produced. It might be a lovely painting, an oriental rug, or a piece of chintz. Picking up the colors and rearranging them becomes a fascinating game.

In planning a color scheme, avoid the use of equal amounts of color. Vary the hue as well as the intensity and value. Choose a basic color and then add small amounts of other hues. Usually it is better to employ bright colors for small areas and grayed or neutral ones for large spaces. Select the colors for the largest area first. Then add the others carefully, one at a time, until the right blend is obtained.

For the best results, make a definite plan. Put swatches of

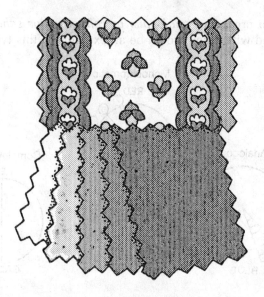

fabrics or colored papers together. Overlap the samples so you can actually see the effect of the colors on each other. Sometimes a quilt artist who is planning the color scheme for a patchwork quilt mounts actual pieces on a felt board so she can be sure the effect is right. If the quilt is to have a border and sashing added, then the colors for these should be considered carefully. Even the lining or underlayer has its place in the color scheme. If you are planning to use an accent color, perhaps in pillows on your sofa, put samples of the new colors next to a swatch of the sofa fabric. It is only by working with colors that you can develop a true color sense.

Certain colors seem to express the personality of a specific decorating period better than others. Brilliant, bold hues, sometimes in combination with or as accents against a white background, seem right for a modern room setting. On the other hand, soft, delicate coloring seems more suitable for a French decor; rich, elegant tones of gold, red, green, and plum for the eighteenth-century English period; clear colors, somewhat muted, of the natural dyes for Early American styles.

Texture and Pattern

Texture and pattern, like line and color, play an important part in planning your quilting project. In fact it is this element that makes the quilting possible. Texture affects both line and color by adding a dimensional quality to them. Because of this, before choosing your fabrics it is best to understand textures and patterns and the illusions they produce.

TEXTURAL EFFECTS

Fabrics can be dull or shiny, smooth or rough, soft or crisp, transparent or opaque. Shiny surfaces that reflect light will make an object appear larger, whereas dull ones make it seem smaller. Smooth surfaces seem to minimize size; rough textures add bulk and weight. Employ these qualities to create the fashion effects you want in your quilting projects.

PATTERNS AT WORK

When discussing lines earlier in this chapter, patterns were mentioned briefly. I touched on the vertical- or horizontal-line direction they might follow, the straight or curved form they might take. There is, however, a great deal more to pattern than just these qualities. See illustration on next page.

Patterns can be small and subdued or large and bold, clear and distinct or muted and whispering, regular or irregular in size. Patterns also seem to have feminine or masculine qualities, contemporary or period moods.

The size and direction of a pattern produce optical illusions. Small, pale, quiet ones seem to make the object smaller, whereas large, clear, colorful designs seem to increase the apparent size. The direction the design takes can guide the eye up or down, in or out.

Small florals, delicate prints, or pale muted designs seem to add a certain feminine charm to a room, whereas bold geometrics make a room seem more masculine. Of course, a feel-

ing of femininity or masculinity in a pattern is also affected by color. A pale pink floral design seems more feminine than the same pattern in a bright orange.

In planning your design, be sure to think about the mood you wish to create. It is best to employ designs that follow the feeling of the room setting. Mixing periods requires experience. As a general rule, geometric designs, bold abstracts, and unusual patterns look right for a contemporary setting. Some of the Amish quilts, with their abstract geometric designs, seem to relate to the contemporary paintings of such artists as Josef Albers. Velvet, satin, moiré, brocade, and damask seem to belong in formal design plans. A crazy quilt made of velvet and satin will appear much more elegant than one made of percale and muslin. Gingham, calico, primitive or hand-woven linen patterns seem to complement an Early American or rustic setting.

If you are a novice at designing and decorating, be conservative about combining patterns. It is difficult to mix them effectively. Using just one print in a room is a safe rule to follow.

Pick up a solid from the print or use a check, stripe, or plaid that blends well with the print.

In planning a quilting design, remember it should complement a room or a person. Its lines, colors, textures, and patterns should blend, setting a pleasing mood. Only when you see them all together, and in the setting where they will be used, will you receive the true picture of the color and fabric scheme.

BEFORE YOU BEGIN

3

Terms to Know

Although this may seem strange, quilters have a language of
their own. Familiar words take on new meanings. Different au-
thors use different terminology. No doubt these differences are
due, in part, to the origin of the work that has been handed
down from country to country, place to place, and generation
to generation.

Before you consider various terms you should understand
the connotation of the word "quilting" itself. Quilting is thought
of in so many ways that it isn't easy to define. If you check
your dictionary, you will find the word defined as a technique
as well as a type of material, which in turn can be referred to
as "quilted." This may cause some confusion, but then there is
the word "quilt" that is identified as a coverlet, as well as the
process for making a special type of material or creating a design detail. Then, to further confound the situation, quilting is
not used just for producing quilts, and not all quilts are made
with quilting.

To pursue this interplay of words even further, a "quilter"
can be the person doing the quilting or a tiny sewing machine
attachment. If these definitions seem perplexing, don't be con-
cerned. Unraveling the various meanings of these words gives
a special interest to this type of needlework. Perhaps it is this
versatility that contributes to quilting's special appeal.

What Is Quilting and What Exactly Is a Quilt?

As a technique, quilting is a form of decorative sewing that is relatively easy to do, consisting of tiny running stitches that hold three layers of material together. The stitches are made by hand or machine, creating a variety of designs. As for the materials, a batting is sandwiched between two pieces of fabric. The top piece can be decorative or plain, depending on the type of quilting you have chosen to do. The bottom layer is usually plain in color. The combination of stitches and materials creates a puffy effect, giving the resulting fabric its distinguishing characteristic. The quilt itself can be used as a bedspread or blanket and it is made to a specific size. (For information on measuring, see page 265.)

Quilted material can be purchased by the yard. However, the choice of fabric and color is limited. Fortunately, when you cannot find what you want, you can make it yourself on the sewing machine or, if you wish, by hand.

WHEN IS A QUILT NOT A QUILT?

There are various types of bedcoverings that feature quilting details, but not all are classified as quilts.

A small version, which does not cover the pillow on the bed but provides warmth, is sometimes called a *throw* or *coverlet*.

A thick version, perhaps three or four inches in depth, is referred to as a *comforter* or *puff*.

An all-white bedcover, which does not have an inner layer of batting, is called a *counterpane*. The two remaining layers, however, are held together with quilting stitches. Sometimes corded and trapunto quilting are used to produce a more decorative effect.

The Special Language of Quilting

If you sew, then you are acquainted with many of the following terms. Today, however, not everyone sews. Because of this, I have given certain definitions so it will be easier to follow the directions in this book. The words are listed in alphabetical order and many of the terms are explained more completely in other parts of the book.

Album Quilt. Just as a photo album has a series of different pictures, so does the album quilt. Instead of pages there are blocks. Usually each one has a different design that may be appliquéd or made of patchwork. Sometimes the quilter uses her favorite flowers and birds for the design motif. Usually the blocks are made by several individuals at home and then assembled and quilted at a get-together with friends.

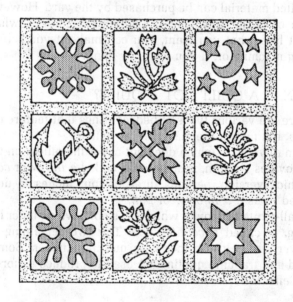

Amish Quilt. These quilts are distinguished by a simplicity of design and a unique use of color that create a strong, striking pattern in deeper tones. Usually the quilting stitches are beautifully made.

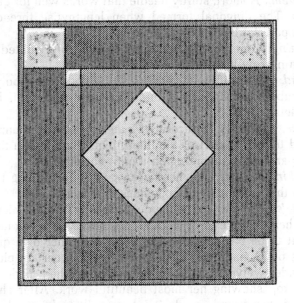

Apartment Quilting. The quilting of individual blocks by using a small ring frame or hoop when the quilter's working quarters aren't big enough to accommodate a large quilting frame.

Appliqué. The application of a small design in one fabric to a larger background piece in another fabric in order to create a decorative motif.

Autograph or Signature Quilt. Written in ink or embroidery stitches, the signatures of friends highlight the design of this type of presentation quilt.

Backing. The bottom layer of quilted material, usually plain in color.

Batt. A roll of fluffy material that is used as the filler when a quilted material is made.

Batting. The fluffy material that is used as the filler when a quilted material is made. Sometimes the words "batt" and "batts" are used in place of batting.

Between. A short, sturdy needle that works well for quilting.

Bias. The diagonal formed when lengthwise threads are placed parallel to crosswise threads.

Binding. A method for finishing the edges of a quilted piece, using a narrow bias strip.

Blend. When different fibers, such as cotton and polyester, are combined in the making of a fabric, the material is known as a blend.

Block. A portion of decorated material, usually square, that is used to form a part of a quilted item. Dividing the top into small parts makes working on a quilt easier to do.

Bodkin. A blunt, flat, needlelike gadget for pulling tape or ribbon through a series of openings or a hem.

Bride's Quilt. An appliquéd quilt with elaborate designs featuring hearts, doves, cupids, and love knots. It was sometimes thought to be bad luck for a bride to make her own quilt, so friends often made one for her. However, in certain places, a girl made twelve quilts for her dowry and then made a thirteenth top showing her most beautiful work. After she was engaged, her friends made it into a quilt to be used on her marriage bed.

Bunching. Rows of contour quilting placed very close together. This creates a beautiful effect, but it is time-consuming to do.

Butted Border. A way to join border strips with vertical or horizontal seams to form a smooth corner as shown here.

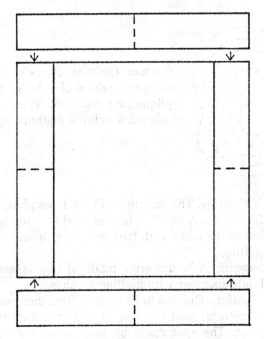

Chiaroscuro. The placement of light and dark elements in a pictorial fashion.

Clip. A small cut or snip in the edge of fabric or thread.

Commemorative Quilt. National interests were usually the subject of these quilts. Flags, patriotic motifs, political symbols, commemorative ribbons, and handkerchiefs were used.

Contour Quilting. Rows of stitches repeating the outline of a design such as an appliqué or patchwork. The rows should be placed a definite distance apart.

Corded Quilting. The insertion of cord to emphasize the outline of the design. A channel for the cord is made by defining the outline of the motif with two rows of stitches. Also called Italian quilting.

Counterpane. A bedcovering made of two layers of white material held together with quilting stitches.

Counterpoints. Quilting in its earliest form consisted of three layers of material held together at certain points with a few firm stitches. The spot made by these anchor stitches is referred to as a counterpoint or quiltpoint.

Crazy Quilt. A pieced quilt that is a combination of appliqué

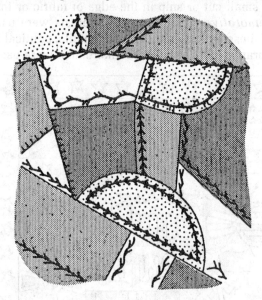

and embroidery. Irregular-shaped scraps of material are sewn to a larger backing piece, forming a collage. Each piece is defined with a row of simple embroidery stitches.

Crosswise Grain. The threads of the fabric that run from selvage to selvage and at right angles to the lengthwise threads.

Easing. A technique used to fit a larger edge to a smaller one. The fabric is manipulated by the fingers.

Echo Quilting. Quilting stitches worked on the background material, following the shape of the design. Echo quilting is frequently used for an appliquéd top. The rows of stitches should be evenly spaced. *See* Contour Quilting.

English Paper Patchwork. This method offers a very precise way of preparing patchwork. A piece of fabric is basted over a piece of paper that has been cut in the required shape. When all of the pieces have been sewn together, the paper is removed.

English Quilting. An embroidered effect obtained by using a backstitch and thick mercerized cotton, creating a solid line.

Family Record Quilt. A type of album quilt with each block picturing a family event.

Filler Pattern. Designs made by the stitches that hold the layers of material together between the major decorative motifs, giving the plain areas a surface interest.

Frame or Border. A band of fabric placed around the edge of a quilt to create an attractive finish. *(See also* page 240.)

Freedom Quilt. One that was given to a young man as a gift on his twenty-first birthday. It had no special feature to distinguish it, but often patriotic motifs and mannish symbols were used.

Friendship Quilt. One made as a gift by a group of friends for someone, perhaps a departing acquaintance, the minister, or a bride. Each block was made by a different person and then quilted by the group at a party or quilting "bee." Embroidered or written signatures or verses were often added. (Next page.)

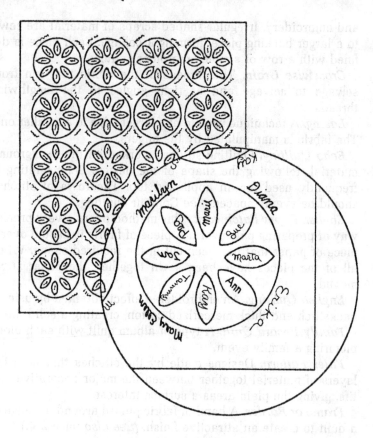

Grain. Fabric woven with two sets of thread, one running vertically, the other horizontally. They must be woven at right angles to each other.

Grid. An arrangement of vertical and horizontal lines forming squares of uniform size. The grid, which can vary in size, is convenient to use when planning a quilting design or enlarging a pattern.

Ground. The background material, to which an appliqué is sewn, may be referred to as the ground.

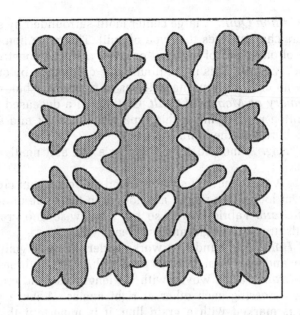

Hawaiian Quilt. You will have no trouble recognizing this type of quilt. The appliquéd designs have the feeling of the lush vegetation of the islands and seem bold because of the contrast in color.

Italian Quilting. Corded quilting is sometimes referred to in this way.

Lap Quilting. A technique by which the three layers are quilted together in small, block-sized units before they are joined to form the larger piece or quilt.

Lattice. Sometimes the blocks are held together with strips of fabric running vertically and horizontally. The crossing of the strips produces a lattice effect.

Lengthwise Grain. The thread that runs parallel to the selvage of the fabric.

Linsey-woolsey. A coarse fabric woven of linen and wool. Probably the first material made in the American colonies.

Marriage Quilt. Another name for a bride's quilt.

Medallion Quilt. A large center motif surrounded by several borders characterizes this type of quilt. The medallion can be made of one piece of material or given a pieced construction.

Medley Quilt. This is an album-type quilt made by one person, who uses her favorite patterns to make each block.

Memory or Memorial Quilt. Clothing of a deceased person was often used to make this type of quilt. Dark and somber colors bordered the quilt.

Mitering. A method for producing a flat and neatly folded corner.

Nap. A fuzzy surface such as found on velvet that creates a different look when pieces are not cut in the same direction.

Off-Grain. Fabric woven so the lengthwise and crosswise threads are not at right angles to each other.

Off Hand. The hand that works under the quilt, guiding the needle and making sure it has passed through the three layers.

On-Grain. Fabric woven with the lengthwise and crosswise threads crossing each other at right angles. When a pattern piece is marked with a grain line, it is important that it be placed exactly on the grain line.

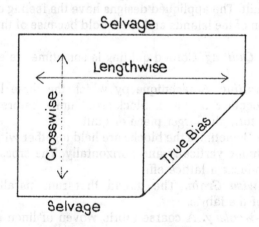

One-way Design. A design printed so the pattern runs in only one direction.

Outline Quilting. The stitches follow the shape of each piece in the design. They are placed a certain distance from the seam lines within each shape. This results in an all-over pattern that can be seen clearly on the back of the quilt.

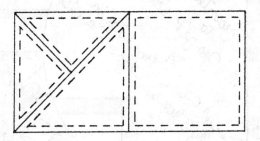

Padding. Soft material such as batting and cord inserted between two layers of material to produce a three-dimensional effect.

Patch. For quilting, a small piece of fabric cut in a specific shape and used as part of a design.

Patchwork. A form of pieced work that follows a geometric design pattern, creating a larger piece of decorative material from smaller ones.

Picture Quilt. The block designs are pictorial, often telling a story. At one time they followed religious or political themes. Now they more often tell a child's story or record historical scenes in a town.

Pieced Work. A larger unit made by sewing small pieces of material together. It has a broader connotation than patchwork. Crazy and strip quilting can fall into this classification.

Piecing. Sewing small pieces of cloth together to make a larger one. The resulting unit is referred to as pieced work. It can be done by hand or machine.

Presentation Quilt. Sometimes a quilt was made for someone who was being honored on a special occasion such as a retirement or promotion. The quilt was made as a group project and presented at a social gathering. Illustration on next page.

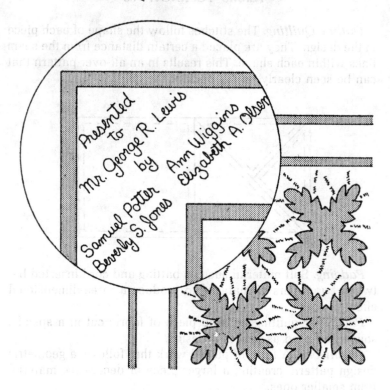

Presented to Mr. George R. Lewis by Samuel Potter Beverly S. Jones Ann Wiggins Elizabeth A. Olson

Quilt. A bed coverlet made with a layer of batting sandwiched between two layers of fabric forming a top and bottom. The three layers are held together by hand or machine stitches that create a decorative pattern.

Quilting. A sewing technique that places tiny running stitches through layers of material to hold them together. This procedure forms a thick fabric with a decorative three-dimensional effect.

Quilt Points. Another term for counterpoints.

Sampler Quilt. As many designs as possible were used, often in an attempt to keep a record or file of various patterns.

Sash Work. Also referred to as lattice strips. The strips are used to join the blocks and, at the same time, frame each one.

Secession Quilt. Made by Southern women who used themes to express their desire for secession at the time of the Civil War. Trapunto quilting was used on white fabric to emphasize the beauty of the design.

Selvage. The finished edges found on woven fabric, running lengthwise.

Seminole Quilting. A form of strip quilting on which brightly colored strips are stitched together to form a wider strip. The

strip is then cut crosswise to form small pieces that are turned and rejoined, creating a patchwork effect with a different look. It is the work of the Seminole Indians.

Set or Setting. The manner by which the decorative blocks are put together to form the quilt top.

Stay-Stitching. A row of machine stitches placed along an edge to hold the piece in shape and prevent the fabric from raveling and stretching.

String Quilting. A type of strip quilting made with very narrow strips of fabric.

Strip Quilting. Strips of fabric sewn together instead of small geometric pieces for pieced work. The resulting strip can be cut into small pieces that are then arranged to form interesting patterns such as for Seminole quilting or used as stitched for a striped effect.

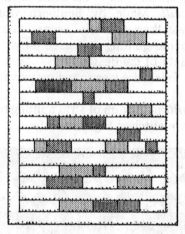

Stuffed Quilting. Trapunto and corded quilting are sometimes referred to in this way.

Template. A pattern guide for marking fabric accurately. It can be made of various materials such as cardboard, sandpaper, and plastic. You can make templates yourself or purchase some of the more popular designs.

Tombstone Quilt. Made in memory of a family member who died, it gave the name, the date of death, and the age.

Top. The uppermost layer of the three used to make a quilt or quilted material.

Trapunto. Small quilted areas stuffed to give a puffed or raised effect to the design.

Tying. The three layers of material can be held together by a series of straight stitches scattered over the quilt. The thread for each stitch is cut and the ends tied in a double or square knot.

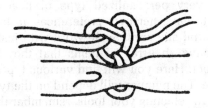

Wedding Quilt. Another term used for a bride's or marriage quilt.

Whole-Cloth Quilt. One made of a single large piece of fabric for the top and embellished with quilting stitches. Usually the fabric is plain in color.

Workt Spread. Linen homespun was marked and sold to be "workt"—another term for "embroidered."

4

What You Will Need to Get Started

Quilting is a very personalized type of needlework. Each quilter seems to have her own preferences as to what equipment and material she uses. Some work with just a few items while others have an array of items that they feel help the resulting product. Here you will find various types from which you can choose. The number will depend on the type of quilting you are doing. In selecting your tools, remember that they influence the quality of work you do, so it is wise to purchase good ones.

You may want to experiment before you select your tools. What works well in one project may not in another. Of course the ones you choose will depend on the type and style of quilting you are doing.

Sewing Tools

No doubt you will find many of the things mentioned here in your sewing basket. There is no reason to buy new ones if you already have ones you can use.

THREAD

Quilting has its own thread. It is a cotton thread with a special coating and is made in a range of colors. Some of the best quilters feel it is a "must" for hand piecing, appliqué, and all hand quilting as well as for machine quilting.

If you find it difficult to find quilting thread, you can use a good, all-purpose thread, number 50. Running it through a cake of beeswax helps to keep the thread from tangling and fraying as you work. If you prefer to do your work by machine, a cotton-covered polyester thread is suitable for piecing and appliqué.

For basting, use a strong thread that can withstand stretching in the hoop and the folding and unfolding of the article. It is most important that the layers of material be held together in the correct position. Basting with a thread in a contrasting color is usually best.

The color of the thread to use for other quilting processes depends on the effect you wish. *For sewing procedures,* matching thread is usually used. *For quilting stitches,* white is usually seen, although you may prefer one that blends or contrasts with the top layer.

Beeswax. For hand sewing, a cake of beeswax or paraffin can be used to wax the thread. Many quilters feel that it strengthens the thread, helps to keep it from knotting, and makes it easier for the thread to slip through the fabric. Be sure not to leave an excess of wax on the thread.

NEEDLE

Just as with thread, there is a special needle known as a quilting needle or a between. It is used to make the tiny stitches for hand quilting.

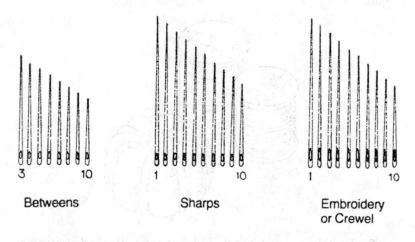

Betweens   Sharps   Embroidery or Crewel

For sewing procedures such as piecing and appliqué, use a long, slender needle called a sharp. It is long enough so that several stitches can be made before the needle is drawn through the material.

For both types of needles, size 8 is a good one to use. If, however, you need a larger, heavier needle for heavier quilt materials, use a number 7, and a smaller, lighter needle for more delicate fabrics in a number 10. Some fabrics are woven more tightly than others. In order to penetrate the fabric, you may have to change the size of the needle.

PINS

There are special pins for quilting. If, however, you are unable to find them, use dressmaker's silk pins. Pins should be smooth, thin, rustproof, with sharp points, and of good quality. Size 17 is a good one to have.

PINCUSHION

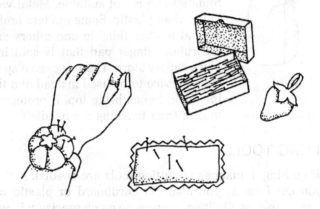

To avoid pricking your fingers and spilling the pins on the floor, you need a pincushion. The type you use depends on personal preference. For sewing procedures, the wrist variety is often the most convenient to use.

THIMBLE

A thimble is really needed for quilting. In fact two thimbles are often necessary—one for the right hand, the other for the left. They keep the fingers from becoming bruised when pushing the needle through the three layers of material. If you are right-handed, you should wear one on the middle finger of your right hand and one on the first finger of your left hand. These

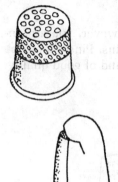

positions should be reversed if you are left-handed.

The thimble should be light in weight, fit the finger comfortably, and be free of rough spots that might snag the fabric and thread. The shape of the thimble for quilting should be considered. The top should be quite flat and the edge well defined. A rounded end is not suitable. Metal works better than plastic. Some quilters prefer a special leather thimble and others use a red rubber finger pad that is sold in an office supply store. There is even a special metal device to be used instead of a thimble. Held beneath the top, it protects the fingers from touching the needle.

CUTTING TOOLS

For quilting, a number of cutting tools are needed. Not only do you cut fabrics, you also cut cardboard or plastic when making templates. Quilting requires so much precision in workmanship that it is important that the tools be good ones and sharp. Certain tools should be kept only for cutting fabrics.

Scissors. There are various types of scissors. Some are made especially for different crafts, including appliqué. No matter what type they are, scissors should have sharp points and narrow blades that fit together tightly. You use them to snip threads and to clip fabric, for example, at corners. Scissors are available in various lengths. They seem to be most useful in the 3- to 5-inch (7.5- to 12.5-cm) length.

Shears. Although scissors are easier to handle than shears because they are lighter, you will need a pair of dressmaker shears to cut fabric. They should always be kept well sharpened. A model with bent handles, about 7 inches (18 cm) long, is a good one to have. If you are left-handed, remember that there are special shears for left-handed people. There is also a type of shears that can accommodate more than one or two

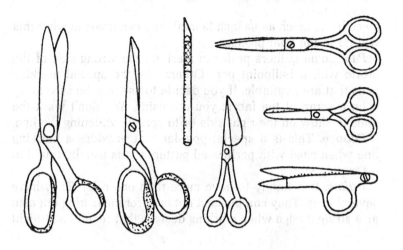

layers with accurate results. You may decide to have a pair of scissors or shears that you use just for cutting paper.

Razor-bladed Knife. This is a handy gadget to have for cutting templates from heavy cardboard. The handle should be narrow so it can be held like a pencil, perpendicular to the edge of the ruler. A favorite type is Exacto. When replacing blades, number 11 is a good choice.

MARKING TOOLS

Because quilting is a precise form of needlework, it is important that the making of templates and the marking of design lines be done with great accuracy and care. Using the correct tools will make this easier to do.

Pencil. A number 2 hard pencil is good for marking. It should have a sharp point so the marked line will be fine and clear, defining the size of the design accurately.

If it is difficult to see the penciled line on the fabric, try a dressmaker's or artist's white drawing pencil. Be sure to keep the point sharp. This isn't always easy: the point becomes blunt quickly and the chalk seems to rub off on the material. A wider line made with a blunt end can increase the size of each piece by as much as 1/8 inch (3 mm). You can imagine what this will do to the final product.

Pen. Some quilters prefer to mark on the wrong side of the fabric with a ballpoint pen. Others like the special marking pens that are available. If you decide to use one, be sure to try it on a scrap of the fabric you are using. You don't want the lines to show on the right side or to spread, widening the line.

Pounce. This is a special powder that provides a marking line when used with perforated patterns. It is usually found in art supply stores.

Rulers. It is handy to have more than one ruler. They have several uses. They can be used not only for measuring but also as a straight edge when marking designs that require a straight

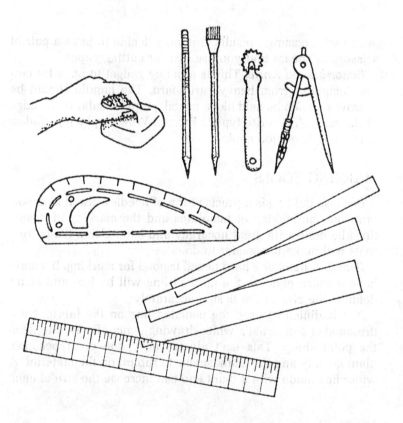

line. It is convenient to have rulers in different sizes and different materials. A 6-inch (15-cm) and a C-Thru ruler, which is 2 by 18 inches (5 by 46 cm), that are transparent and flexible, are handy to have. A 24-inch (61-cm) ruler with a metal edge or one made of all metal works well when marking straight quilting patterns, for example, on a quilt top or when making templates.

Compass. This is handy to have when drawing curves.

Fusible Material. For a few basic patchwork shapes, it is possible to purchase a pattern on a sheet of fusible material. After fusing the sheet to the quilting fabric, the shapes can be cut out on the premarked lines.

Designing Aids

You can purchase designs for various types of quilting. Templates, perforated patterns, stencils, hot-iron patterns, and kits are available. Often these patterns are limited in design, making it impossible for you to find one you like. If you decide to create your own design, you will need some special aids.

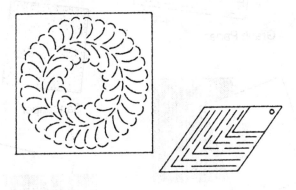

MATERIALS

Graph Paper. This type of paper is available in various sizes for planning designs. One with 4 squares to the inch (2.5 cm) and in a sheet 17 by 22 inches (43 by 56 cm) is handy to use.

Cardboard. To make templates and other pattern designs, use a sturdy, stiff, single-thickness cardboard such as an artist's illustration board, which is easy to handle and durable.

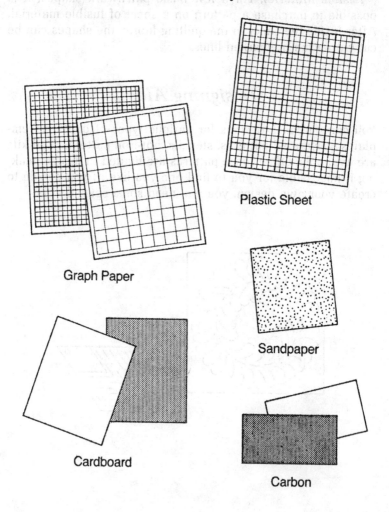

Plastic Sheet

Graph Paper

Sandpaper

Cardboard

Carbon

This is an important point to remember. The size and shape of the pattern must remain the same no matter how many times it is used. The edges must remain smooth, never becoming rough or frayed.

Dressmaker's Carbon. This is convenient for transferring design markings.

Plastic Sheet. This can be used for pattern designs. Some of the sheets are marked as graph paper is.

Fabrics for Quilting

Selecting materials for quilting isn't as easy as it might seem. Fabric of 100 percent cotton, which seems best for quilting, is often difficult to find. In making your selection, the item you are creating, the pattern, and the manner of construction will influence your choice.

In the early days of quilting, the ragbag was the source of many of the fabrics. Scraps of cloth left after making the family clothes were tucked into a bag for future use. Nothing was thrown away.

Today that method of fabric selection is seldom used. New fabrics are purchased for the project. Finding fabric with the right fiber content in the right type, weight, and color can be a problem. When several fabrics are being used, such as in a patchwork design, the trouble is compounded. It is important that the materials you use be of good quality and that they be right for each other, the design, and the manner of construction. For example, whether you are making a quilt or a wall hanging, an heirloom piece or a pot holder, using machine or hand stitches will determine the kind of fabric used. In most needlework, the selection of one fabric is sufficient, but not for quilting. Each of the three layers must be given careful consideration. Although the top and bottom layers may be similar, the in-between layer is very different.

Top Layer. This is the display or decorative side of the quilted item. A solid-colored material as well as a printed one can be used, or the top can be embellished with decorative designs such as appliqué, patchwork, or embroidery. Which-

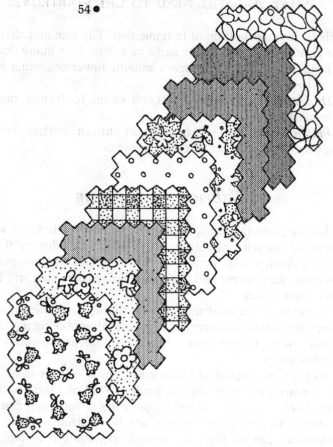

ever type it is, the fabric you use should be of the best quality you can afford. It should be light to medium in weight, easy for the needle to penetrate, and opaque so the seams won't show. A 100-percent cotton broadcloth is usually thought to be the easiest to handle. Percale, calico, chambray, and muslin are other suitable selections, as are fine linen-weave material and flannel for some projects. A tightly woven percale is usually easier to handle by machine than by hand.

For certain designs, those found in a crazy quilt for instance, elegant fabrics such as velvet, satin, and other silks can be used. Sometimes sheers such as voile, organdy, and organza can be used as an overlay on an opaque fabric for a soft or filmy effect, perhaps for a picture or a wall hanging. Stiff and heavy material should be avoided.

Sheets are a good source of material. They are available in a wide range of colors and designs. Because of their width, it is possible to have a top and bottom layer without seams.

When shopping for fabrics be sure to check the fiber content. Although 100-percent cotton seems best, it is not always possible to find it in the color and print you want. At such times a cotton blend can be used, but it will be best to make the entire project out of the same type of material. In this way, you know that the wearing, cleaning, and sewing characteristics will be the same.

Testing the fabric for shrinkage, fastness of color, and pressing before it is used is a good idea. All-cotton fabrics usually shrink and so should be laundered before beginning a project. If the fabric bleeds when being washed, you should note the temperature of the water. Sometimes a cooler water will keep the colors from running. Pressing an all-cotton fabric will require a warmer iron than synthetics do. If the material you are using is a combination of fibers, then you will have to handle it carefully.

Bottom Layer. The backing is usually not as decorative as the top layer. It used to be made of practical material such as muslin or sometimes even flour sacks. Today, however, that practice has disappeared. The lining fabric is usually similar to the top in quality, type, and style. It is generally plain in color, although sometimes a patterned material is used. If you are planning to use the backing to finish the edges, you should choose the material with an eye to its effect with the top. The backing should also be preshrunk if necessary.

Inner Layer. Between the top and bottom layers of this fabric sandwich there is a filling. Although it adds warmth to the quilted project, it also adds a three-dimensional effect that creates a beauty all its own.

The batting should be chosen carefully to produce the effect you desire. Some types of batting create a puffier look than others do. Cotton batting was used in the nineteenth and early twentieth centuries. With the advent of synthetics, polyester

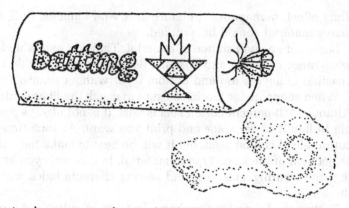

batting became popular. Today both types are available.

The batting is rolled into batts. Batting sheets can be purchased in various sizes and in different thicknesses. Select one that is large enough so it can be used in one piece. Not all battings are of the same quality, so do choose carefully. You may want to try different ones just to be sure you know which one you prefer for certain effects.

Cotton batting provides a lightweight, warm, washable, easy-to-quilt filling. You should remember, however, that this type of batting requires more quilting lines to hold it in place than other battings do. Cotton batting seems to shift and bunch in laundering when not quilted sufficiently. The space between the rows of quilting stitches should not be greater than 2 inches (5 cm). The batting does not seem to shift, though, after it is basted in place and the layers placed in a hoop or frame.

Polyester batting also offers a lightweight, warm, and washable filling that is easy to work with. Because of its stable nature it requires fewer stitches to hold it in place and to keep it from separating when laundered. This type of batting seems to produce a puffier surface, with the stitching lines more clearly defined.

Bonded batting is another type. A treatment has been used to make the batting easier to handle. It also keeps the polyester fibers from slipping through the fabric and creating a linty finish.

Other fillings can be used. Some quilters like to use other fillers for special effects. Wool batting, polyester fleece, cotton flannel, and a blanket have possibilities. A loose stuffing instead of a sheet of batting is sometimes suitable. It is available in cotton and polyester. Under certain conditions, you may want to try kapok and shredded foam.

Although the batts are made in a variety of sizes, it is sometimes impossible to get one just the correct size. If one batt is too small, join two batts to obtain one of the correct dimensions. In case the sheet is too large, of course it can be cut to the correct size.

Whichever filling you decide to use, it will be helpful if you keep a record of the filling and the effect obtained. Also note the amount of batting you needed.

Frames and Hoops

Perfect quilting stitches are easier to make if the layers are held taut and both hands are free, so a frame or a hoop can be used.

THE FRAME

The frame was designed to hold the work taut and in alignment during the quilting. The quilters did not want the three layers to shift their positions, bunch up, or wrinkle.

In the beginning, the frame was simple in construction; just four poles were held together at the corners with pegs or clamps. The poles ranged in length from 6 to 10 feet (180 to 300 cm). The frame rested on its own stand or sometimes on sawhorses at the corners or even the backs of wooden chairs. Eight to sixteen quilters could find places around the frame. You might think that it would be difficult to make tiny stitches under such conditions, but it almost seems that the stitches the quilters made were smaller than those made today. While quilting, their arms rested on the crossbars. Thread and scissors were kept handy by placing them on the surface of the material.

Today the quilting frame is still a functional piece of equipment. It hasn't changed too much in structure and can still be

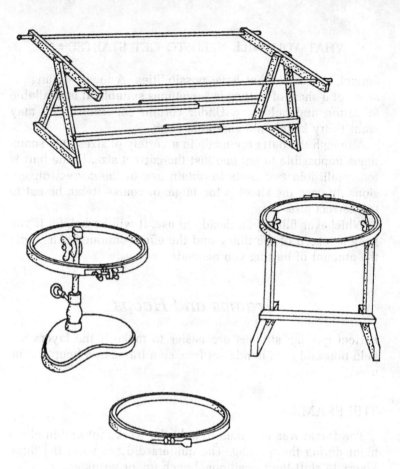

made at home. Its popularity has slipped, however, because of its size. Not too many people have an area large enough to accommodate a frame. They cannot allow the frame to remain up until the quilting is completed. Once a quilt is placed on a frame, it is better that it remain there until the work is completed. And this can take quite a bit of time.

If you do have the space, then you will find a frame very handy when quilting a large piece of material. Today commercial frames are available in different sizes and styles. Several of them can be folded so they are easy to store between uses. Before you purchase one, be sure to check the different types so you will find one that suits your needs and is convenient to handle.

THE HOOP

The wooden hoop, which is smaller and portable, can be used in place of a frame. It should be round. Oval ones do not seem to allow the material to be held with an even tension.

Hoops vary in size. A large one, which can be adapted for projects in various sizes, is best to use. One about 23 inches (56 cm) in diameter works nicely. You can even quilt an entire quilt on this type of hoop.

In order to regulate the tightness by which the layers are held in place, the outer hoop should be constructed with small wooden blocks through which a long bolt is slipped. Some hoops are made with a stand to which the inner hoop is attached. This is a good type to use because it allows both of your hands to be free to make the stitches. If your hoop doesn't have a stand, you can support it on a table or chair while quilting.

5

Sew to Quilt

Quilting, as I've said, is a decorative form of sewing. Simple sewing techniques are used to create the lovely effects found in quilted materials. Small stitches and neat seams, worked with precision, are the basis for beautiful quilted articles. On the following pages you will find a description of sewing procedures to use in preparing types of quilted materials. If you are not familiar with any of the techniques, be sure to practice the process before you actually use it.

For some reason sewing is not always associated with quilt making. But if you consider it a moment you will realize that the foundation for quilting is really sewing. The same simple techniques are used for both. The perfection of the stitches and seams is most important. Precision in each procedure cannot be stressed too much. Without it, the beauty of quilting cannot be achieved.

For years, quilts and quilted materials were made by hand. The quilter took great pride in her ability to make exquisite stitches. Gradually the sewing machine has taken the place of hand sewing in quilt making, just as it has in other types of sewing. In many instances, a combination of hand and machine stitches is used.

Hand Sewing Stitches

Delicate hand stitches are a "must." They increase the beauty and value of a quilted article. To be sure that the stitches are as perfect as possible, it is important that you learn to handle sewing equipment and materials correctly. And though some of the following suggestions may seem unnecessary, they really aren't. Threading the needle, for example, and how you hold it may affect the final look.

TECHNIQUES

Begin by selecting the thread and needle carefully. Both should be the type and size that are correct for the work. Cut the thread diagonally from the spool about 20 inches (51 cm) long. Put this end through the eye of the needle. Usually a single thread is used for the stitches.

Sewing stitches are usually made from right to left unless one is left-handed. Begin the sewing on the right-hand end close to the edge. Secure the thread in one of two ways, whichever seems better for your work. For the first, take two or three tiny stitches, one on top of the other. For the second, use a knot at the end of the thread. When a knot is used for a permanent stitch, be sure it does not show. For quilting, it can be hidden between the layers of fabric.

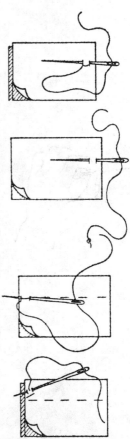

End by sewing the thread firmly but inconspicuously. Make two or three small stitches in the same place if the stitches are permanent ones. Sometimes this procedure is followed by two or three running stitches.

When working with temporary stitches such as basting, place two or three separate backstitches in a diagonal direction. Be sure the last stitch is close to the edge.

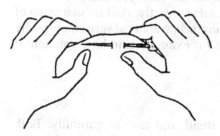

Holding the article and needle correctly makes sewing easier and quicker to do. Usually it is best if the bulk of an article is held toward you. It seems to make it easier to guide the position and size of the stitches.

Grasp the material with the left hand between the thumb and first finger, with the thumb on top and the needle in the right hand. In this position, the left hand controls the fabric and the right hand guides the needle.

To hold the needle properly, put it between the thumb and the first finger so that it touches the side of the thimble near the tip. This allows the middle finger to push the needle through the fabric with ease. Although many sewers work without a thimble, they really shouldn't. It is impossible to make perfect little stitches without one. It is especially important to use a thimble when quilting. Without it, the finger becomes sore and the skin punctured. Once you become used to wearing a thimble, you will work faster and with greater precision.

The hand sewing stitches used most often for quilting projects are listed here in alphabetical order so you can refer to them quickly.

Backstitch. Some quilters like to use this stitch because it produces such a strong seam. On the upper side, the stitches resemble a line of machine stitches.

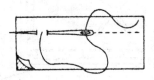

To make the stitch, bring the needle up on the seam line. Return the needle to the fabric 1/16 inch (1.5 mm) to the right. Slip the needle under the fabric, coming up 1/8 inch (3 mm) to the left.

Insert the needle in the material at the start of the first stitch, making another 1/16 inch (1.5 mm) long. Continue this process, moving backward and forward, forming a continuous row of stitches.

Basting. This is a temporary stitch, but an important one in quilting. It is used in many ways, such as to hold folded edges and layers of material in place. The stitches can be even or uneven in length, and straight or diagonal in direction. Sew with thread in a contrasting color; it is easier to remove these temporary stitches at the proper time.

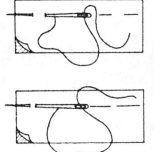

Even basting is used when there is strain on the area to be sewn. Begin with a knot at the end of the thread. The stitches should be 1/4 inch (6 mm) long and 1/4 inch (6 mm) apart. Finish the row of stitches with two or three backstitches. When you remove them, cut the thread at frequent intervals.

Uneven basting makes a good guideline when a marking line is needed. It also holds layers of material together when there is little strain. Take a long stitch on the upper side and a short stitch on the under one.

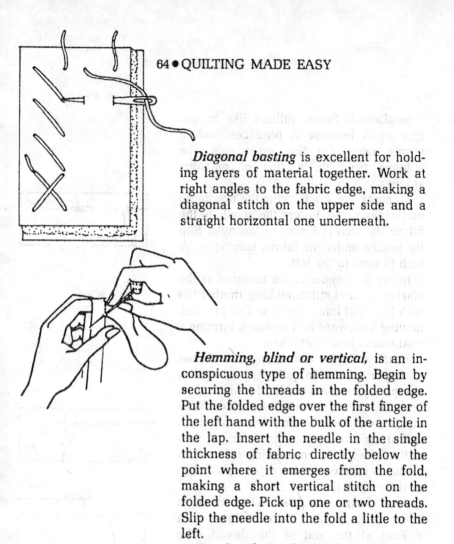

Diagonal basting is excellent for holding layers of material together. Work at right angles to the fabric edge, making a diagonal stitch on the upper side and a straight horizontal one underneath.

Hemming, blind or vertical, is an inconspicuous type of hemming. Begin by securing the threads in the folded edge. Put the folded edge over the first finger of the left hand with the bulk of the article in the lap. Insert the needle in the single thickness of fabric directly below the point where it emerges from the fold, making a short vertical stitch on the folded edge. Pick up one or two threads. Slip the needle into the fold a little to the left.

Overhand Stitch. Used to hold two finished edges of fabric together. The stitches appear straight on the upper side and slanting on the under. It produces a strong, invisible seam that can be opened out flat.

Fold under the edges the required width. With the right sides together and finished edges matching, sew the sections together. Pass the needle straight through the back fold and then through the front fold with the needle pointing toward you. Pick up one or two threads in the folds. Place the stitches close together as you continue to work to the left.

Running Stitch. This is most important for quilting. Sometimes it is referred to as the quilting stitch. It really is a tiny form of the basting stitch. The stitches are 1/16 to 1/8 inch (1.5 to 3 mm) long. After securing the end of the thread, pick up a small amount of material with the needle. Weave the needle in and out of the cloth until there are several stitches on it. Pull the needle through the material. You are now ready to start the next series of stitches.

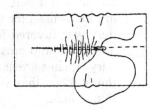

Slip Stitch. Worked on the right side, but it cannot be seen on the right side. On the underside, the stitches appear as regular basting. Fold under the edge the required amount. Press or baste. Place the folded edge over the under piece. Fasten the thread at the right-hand end with a stitch in the lower section. Slip the needle into the upper section in the fold line. Take a 1/4-inch (6-mm) stitch, inserting the needle in the lower section directly below the point where it emerged. Continue this way, making a stitch first in the lower material and then in the upper.

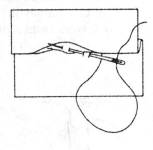

Whipstitch. Resembles the overhand stitch. In fact it is often used in place of it. Two finished or folded edges are sewn together, forming a tiny, firm seam.

Put together the right sides of the sections to be joined. Take a small stitch over the edges, picking up one or two threads of the fabric. To make the next stitch, slip the needle through the material in a slanting position.

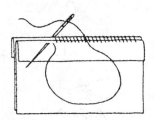

Embroidery Stitches

At various periods in quilting history embroidery has played an important part. The stitches that come to mind most often are those used for the crazy quilt. At one time crewel embroidery was favored for these quilts. Today simple stitches such as outline and cross are most often seen. Sometimes embroidery stitches are used to hold appliqué motifs in place. Some of the stitches that you might find interesting to use are mentioned here.

In case you have never done any embroidery, a few suggestions may be helpful. Usually embroidery stitches are made from left to right instead of the right-to-left direction used for sewing. Of course, if you are left-handed, you will proceed in the opposite direction from a right-handed person. In case you are using a sewing stitch such as the running stitch, then you will work from right to left.

TECHNIQUES

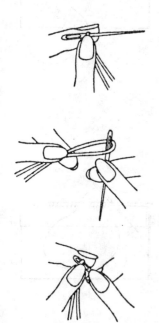

Threading a Needle. Even the threading of a needle should be given special attention. Cut the thread from the spool or skein about 18 inches (45 cm) long. A longer thread often becomes tangled before it is completely used. Thread the needle with the cut end. If you have to separate 6-strand floss, handle it carefully to avoid snarling it.

It is often difficult to thread a needle with a heavy thread or yarn. If this happens, try this method. Put the yarn around the eye of the needle. Hold it firmly, close to the needle. Remove the needle, continuing to squeeze the yarn tightly to flatten it. If you have long fingernails, this isn't always easy to do. Bring the eye of the needle down over the folded yarn a short distance. When you are sure the yarn is entirely through the eye, release the pressure and pull the yarn through the eye.

Beginning. The starting point should be concealed as much as possible. Two or three tiny running stitches made toward the starting place (A) with a very small backstitch (B) anchoring the thread in place works nicely. This allows the embroidery stitch to be made in the correct direction. As the embroidery progresses, the running stitches are covered. For the left-handed person, the stitches should begin as in (C).

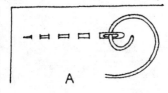

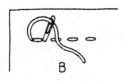

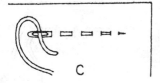

Sometimes a small knot is used if the back of the work will not be seen. The end can be covered by tucking it under a stitch.

Holding the Needle. Grasp the needle between the thumb and first finger so the needle touches the tip of the second finger, which should be wearing a thimble. It is difficult to make tiny stitches without a thimble, and almost impossible to send the needle through three thicknesses of material without injuring the tip of your finger. The only exception to this rule is when the needle moves in a stabbing fashion, up and down in a separate motion.

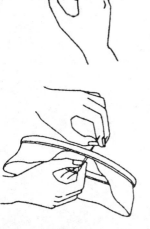

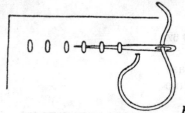

Ending. It is important that the thread be fastened on the wrong side so it is inconspicuous. There are several ways to do this. Always select the one that seems best for the work you are doing. Run the needle under the last two or three stitches. To make the ending more secure, take a tiny backstitch over the last stitch before weaving the needle in and out through the embroidery. Another method uses two tiny backstitches over and under the last stitch and the thread is clipped close.

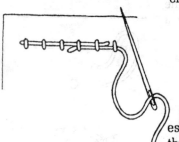

Starting a New Thread. When it is necessary to introduce a new length of thread, it should be done so you cannot detect the joining. Slip the needle under several stitches on the wrong side so the new thread will be held in place. Then bring the thread to the right side at the place where the next stitch is to be made.

Backstitch. Lines and outlines can be embroidered attractively with this stitch, which is also used for sewing. It is important that the stitches be kept even in size and placement to produce a machine-stitching effect.

Start at the right-hand end of the line to be embroidered. Bring the needle to the right side of the material, a stitch length from the end (A). Return the needle to the fabric at the end (B). Let the needle reappear at C, picking up twice the amount of material as covered by the first stitch. To make the second stitch, insert needle at A, carrying thread back to this point. Continue to work in this manner.

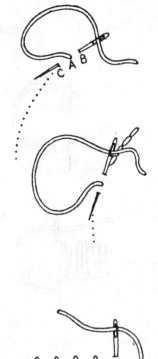

Blanket Stitch. A variety of effects can be made with this stitch. By changing the length and direction of the stitches, as well as the space between, you can produce interesting effects for lines and outlines. It is often used to hold edges in place, as for an appliqué. Working between two guidelines is helpful. They allow you to maintain a regularity in the stitches, which is most important.

Embroider from left to right. Bring the needle to the right side of the material on the lower line or through the edge of the design. Hold the thread in place with the left thumb. Insert the needle at the upper line a short distance to the right, letting it emerge directly below in the lower line. Pull the thread through the loop that has been formed. You are ready to make the next stitch.

Buttonhole Stitch. The procedure for working this stitch is the same as for the blanket stitch. Buttonhole stitches, however, are worked close together, forming a solid design, whereas blanket stitches are separated to produce an open effect. To ensure that the length of the stitches remains the same, use two guidelines.

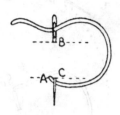

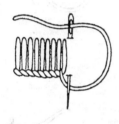

Start at the left-hand end of the lower line (A). Hold the thread down with the left thumb. Insert the needle in the upper line (B) slightly to the right, letting it reappear on the lower line directly under B and close to the place where it first appeared (C). Pull the needle through the loop that has been made. Take the next stitch close to the first one.

If you are using this stitch to finish an edge and the fabric frays easily, work the stitches before cutting out the design. The design, however, can be cut out if the cloth does not ravel. The stitches will then be worked over the raw edge. In either case it is wise to define the outline of the design with running stitches. They will be covered by the buttonhole stitch.

Chain Stitch. This stitch has many uses. It can be employed to mark design lines or borders, as well as for a filling and padding stitch when a raised effect is required. The effect on the underside is that of backstitches.

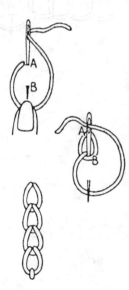

Start by bringing the needle to the right side of the fabric (A). Hold the thread in place with the left thumb so a loop can be formed as the needle is returned to the starting point (A). Insert the needle, bringing it up a short distance below at B. Of course this point will be determined by the desired length of the stitch. Pull the thread through the loop. Be sure not to pull it tight.

For the next stitch, insert the needle inside the loop at the point where the thread emerges (B). The stitches should be kept equal in size.

The chain stitch can be the basis of several embroidery stitches. Two of them are mentioned here—the lazy daisy or detached chain stitch and the magic chain or checkered stitch.

Lazy Daisy Stitch. This is the term most frequently used for the detached chain. The stitch can appear as single ones scattered over an area or grouped together to form a decorative effect as in a floral motif. Sometimes the stitch is combined with the fly stitch to create the effect of a flower.

Make a single chain stitch. Bring the needle to the right side of the material. Hold down the thread with the left thumb so that a loop can be made. Insert the needle at the point where the thread emerged (A). Bring it up a short distance below this spot. After pulling the thread through the fabric, forming the stitch, insert the needle again, taking a small stitch over the end of the loop. This tiny stitch anchors the chain stitch.

Magic Chain Stitch. When worked with two threads in contrasting colors a row of chain stitches takes on a special look. By manipulating the threads, one seems to disappear as a stitch is made, allowing the colors to alternate as the stitches are made.

Start by threading the needle with two threads of contrasting color. Begin as for a chain stitch by bringing the threads to the

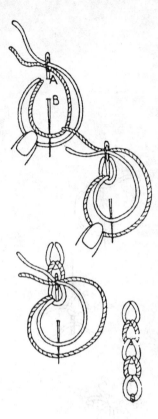

right side. Hold both threads down with the thumb. Make a loop by inserting the needle at A, allowing it to emerge at B.

At this point, do not draw the needle over both threads. Instead put one of the threads, perhaps the lighter, above the needle, allowing the darker one to remain below. This makes it possible for the stitch to be made with only one thread. As you pull the threads through the loop, you will notice that the one above the needle seems to disappear.

The second stitch is made in the same manner, but with the darker thread now above the needle so the lighter thread can be used to make the stitch. As you work, be careful that the thread you are not using is pulled to the wrong side.

Couching. One or more threads are held in place by a series of tiny stitches for couching. This produces an interesting effect when used for lines and borders, as well as for the appliqué designs.

Start by bringing the thread or threads through the fabric at the right-hand end of the line to be covered. Lay them along the design line, holding them in place with your thumb.

Let the couching thread emerge near the end of the line (A) and close to and below the laid threads. Make a small vertical stitch, moving upward over the threads. Slip the needle a short distance to the left under the material, reappearing and ready to take the next stitch. As you work, hold the loose threads firmly so they do not move out of place and pucker. Pull the small stitches taut.

Cross Stitch. This is one of the simpler stitches to make. It is important that the regularity of the stitches be maintained. The length and the slant of the stitches must be even to ensure the beauty of the stitches.

When working on fabric, the stitches are easier to make if the design has been stamped on the material. The stitches, however, can be made by counting threads or working on gingham.

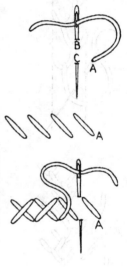

Instead of doing one cross stitch at a time, it is best to work two separate rows of single diagonal stitches. Begin by bringing up the needle at the lower right-hand corner of the line to be covered (A). Insert the needle diagonally above at B, coming up directly below at C, keeping the needle in a vertical fashion. The length and direction of the stitch determine the size of the resulting cross stitch. Continue in this way until the row of single diagonal stitches is finished.

For the second row of slanting stitches, work from left to right, crossing those in the first row and keeping the needle vertical as you work.

Feather Stitch. It is used for lines that may be straight or curved, and as a border to decorate a wide variety of items from baby clothes to crazy quilts. The stitch is worked like a blanket stitch but on an angle, creating a zigzag effect.

It is best to work between two parallel

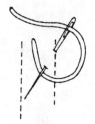

guidelines placed on either side of the line to be decorated. Let the needle emerge at the top of the line to be covered. Hold down the thread with the left thumb. Make a diagonal stitch to the right and slightly below the point where the needle emerged, pointing the needle toward the design line. Pull the needle through the loop, over the working thread.

For the second stitch, loop the thread to the left-hand side of the line. Slip the needle diagonally under the fabric, pointing it toward the design line. Pull the needle through as you did for the first stitch. Alternate the stitches from right to left as you continue. Be sure to keep the stitches the same in size and an equal distance from the line to be covered.

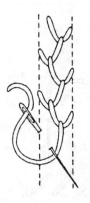

Double Feather Stitch. This is a decorative and popular variation of the feather stitch. Instead of taking a single stitch on the right-hand side and then one on the left, several stitches can be used. Obtain the effect you want by working two, three, or more stitches on one side, and then an equal number on the other side.

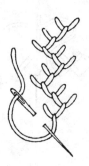

Single Feather Stitch. Although this stitch is made as a one-sided feather stitch, it resembles a blanket stitch in appearance. It can be used for lines and is frequently seen as a decorative touch on smocking.

The needle should emerge at the top of

the line to be covered. Hold the thread
down with the left thumb as you take a
blanket-type stitch to the right and a little
below this point. Keep the needle in a diagonal position, letting it emerge on the
line to be covered. Draw the thread
through the loop and over the working
thread. Continue in this way to make the
remaining stitches.

Fly and Y Stitch. This stitch is a variation of the open detached chain stitch. Instead of the curved U effect this one resembles a V. A loop is held in place by a
vertical stitch, drawing the V into position. The length of this stitch can vary.
When the stitch is long, it is called a Y
stitch. The stitches can be used in various
ways, such as in rows or scattered in an
open pattern as a filling or with another
stitch.

To make the stitch, bring up the needle
at a point that will be the top of the left
arm of the V (A). Hold down the thread
with the left thumb. Insert the needle at
the top of the right arm (B). Slip the needle
diagonally under the material, letting it
emerge at a center point (C), which will
be the base of the V. Be sure to take the
stitch deep enough so the V effect is produced.

Draw the needle through the loop.
Carry it over the thread, letting it reenter
the material just below this point, making
a straight stitch to hold down the loop. In
case you wish the stitch to have more of a
Y appearance, the vertical stitch can be
lengthened.

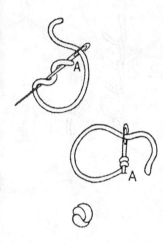

French Knot. These beadlike dots give a three-dimensional effect to an embroidered area. They can be used as a filling for a small area, such as the center of a floral design.

The size of the knot can vary. The weight of the thread and the number of times the thread is wound around the needle make the difference. Sometimes one twist is enough. Although it is possible to make these variations, the beauty of the knot depends on your ability to keep the thread taut around the needle. It will help if you choose your needle carefully. It should be large enough to allow the thread to be drawn easily through the coiled thread and, at the same time, maintain its tightness.

To make the stitch, bring up the needle at the place where the knot is to be made (A). Hold the thread firmly between the left thumb and the first finger quite close to the material. Twist the thread around the needle. Keep it taut. Turn the needle in the opposite direction, inserting it close to the spot where the thread emerged. Draw the needle through the coiled thread to the underside of the work.

Herringbone Stitch. If you sew, you know this stitch as the catch stitch. The appearance of the stitch can be varied by changing the length and direction. Although it is an easy stitch to make, it is important that the stitches be kept even. Its beauty depends on regularity.

Working between two guidelines, proceed from left to right. Bring up the needle at the lower end of the first stitch (A).

Carry the thread diagonally to the upper line. Insert the needle a short distance to the right (B).

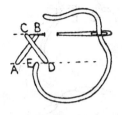

Slide the needle horizontally under the material, bringing it up a short distance to the left (C). Insert it in the lower line (D), carrying the thread over the first stitch. This makes the second diagonal stitch the same length as the first.

To begin the third diagonal stitch, bring the needle to the surface a short distance to the left (E). Be sure to keep the stitches as well as the spacing between the stitches even in length. Notice that ends B and C on the upper line are centered between points A and D on the lower line. Proceed in this manner.

Double Herringbone Stitch. To give the herringbone stitch a more decorative effect, try this variation. Begin with a row of regular herringbone stitches, but be sure to leave a space wide enough between the stitches to insert another one. Use a contrasting thread for the second row of stitches to create an interesting look. The interlacing occurs at the point where the threads cross each other. It is important that the stitches follow a regular direction and sequence at the crossing points.

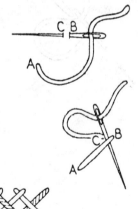

Outline Stitch. As its name implies, this stitch makes a good line for defining a design. It is similar to the stem stitch. The only difference between the two stitches is the placement of the working thread.

Work from left to right. Bring up the needle at the end of the straight or curved line to be covered (A). Insert it a short distance to the right (B), keeping the thread above the needle. Let the needle reappear between A and B at C. For the second stitch, bring up the needle at B. Continue this way.

Running Stitch. This is a very simple stitch to make. It can be used as an important sewing and quilting stitch or for a decorative effect. When using it for embroidery, there must be a definite regularity to the stitches. The running stitch can be used to outline a design or as a foundation for one of the composite stitches.

Usually the stitches are made by picking up and passing over an equal number of threads. There are times, however, when a different effect is desired. Then only one or two threads are picked up on the underside.

As in sewing, the work is done from right to left. Several stitches may be held on the needle before the thread is pulled through the material.

Satin Stitch. Although simple, this stitch requires a great deal of skill to make. The edge of the design must be kept even and well defined to ensure the beauty of the design. This demands careful attention to details. Working between two guidelines will be helpful. The length of the stitch can vary, but it is wise to avoid long stitches that separate easily.

The stitches can be made in a straight or diagonal direction, but they must always be worked close together to produce the satiny look. If a raised effect is needed, pad the design before beginning to make the satin stitches. This can be done by using closely placed running or chain stitches.

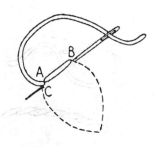

To make the satin stitch, bring the needle to the upper side in the left-hand guideline (A). Draw the thread across the design, putting the needle in the right-hand line (B). Slip the needle under the material, bringing it up on the left side (C) just below A. Continue to work this way until the design area is covered. Make sure that the stitches are close together, not overlapping, and flat.

Split Stitch. This stitch creates the look of a chain stitch. Its construction, however, seems to relate to the stem stitch. It gives an interesting outline to a design. To produce the correct effect, it is necessary to use a thread or yarn that splits easily.

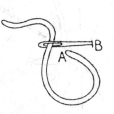

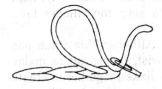

Stem Stitch. This stitch is sometimes called a stalk stitch and closely resembles the outline stitch. It is an easy one to make. The solid line it produces is effective for outlining a design or providing a

foundation for other stitches. The width of the line can be changed by varying the direction of the stitches.

The work is done from left to right with the thread kept below or to the right of the needle. Let the needle emerge at the end of the line to be covered. Insert it a short distance to the right, bringing it up halfway between these two points. Generally the needle enters the fabric below the line, coming up above it a short distance to the left. This gives the stitch a slight slanting look. However, the stitch can be made in a straight line with the needle entering and emerging directly on the line, which creates a narrower effect.

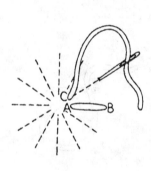

Straight Stitch. For a single, detached flat or satin stitch, use this one. It can vary in length and direction. It should not be used for curving or long lines, but it is effective when used for short lines or grouped with other stitches to form a design such as a star or flower.

The stitch is made by bringing up the needle at A, inserting it at B, and then coming up at C in order to make the next stitch. Be sure to keep the stitches taut, not loose.

Sword Stitch. Although this stitch has an interesting twist, it is easy to make. Two stitches are linked together to create the effect. It makes a pleasing filling or line stitch.

Four points are important to the look of the stitch. Their placement should be planned before the embroidery begins. They determine the width and length of the stitch. The three top points form a triangle with A, the slanting point opposite, and in line with C and B, falling between these two points but above them. Then below B is D, which marks the end of the stitch. For the right look, this section of the stitch should be longer than the other arms are.

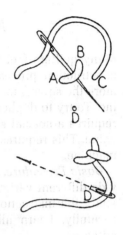

Begin at A by bringing up the needle at this point. Insert the needle at B and come up at C. Leave the stitch between A and B slightly loose so you can get the effect shown here. Pass the needle over and under this stitch, inserting it at D. Give the thread a little tug so the arms of the "sword" fall into place. Start the next stitch to the left of the first one. Continue in this way.

Tête-de-boeuf Stitch. Detached chain and straight stitches can be combined to create an attractive filling stitch. Their placement can produce many attractive looks. One of the most pleasing effects is created when the stitches are arranged in alternating rows to produce diagonal rows.

Start with a detached chain stitch. Do this by bringing up the needle at A. Insert the needle again at A, allowing the thread to form a loop. Bring the needle up again at B. Draw it through the loop. Make a small vertical stitch over the loop, inserting the needle at C. This stitch holds the loop in place.

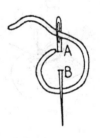

Place a diagonal stitch on each side of the detached chain stitch. Keep the length of the stitches the same, making sure that they give a balanced look to the finished stitch.

Machine Stitches

Many quilters feel that it is a waste of time to do all of the construction processes in quilt making by hand. More and more the sewing machine is being used for contemporary quilting. To try to duplicate the beautiful work found in old quilting requires a special skill in the manipulation of the sewing machine. This requires practice and a thorough knowledge of the machine.

Basic Procedures. Different makes of sewing machines provide different varieties of features. This makes it necessary to study the instruction manual that accompanies your machine carefully. Learn all about your machine before starting to stitch.

Practice starting and stopping, turning corners, maneuvering around curves, and stitching in a perfectly straight line. Unless you have control of your machine, it is impossible to stitch successfully.

Starting. Thread the machine correctly. This is most important. If you don't, you will have a mass of tangled threads. Bring the bobbin thread to the working area by lowering and raising the needle just once. Jerk the upper thread slightly so that a loop of the bobbin thread appears. Put a pin or the points of your scissors through the loop and pull up the end.

To be sure that the needle will not become unthreaded when the first stitch is taken, bring the take-up lever to its highest position. Move the thread ends under the presser foot and back. Be sure that the ends are long enough so they will not become tangled.

Slip the material under the presser foot with the bulk of it to the left. Don't let it hang down. If you do, it will be difficult to stitch accurately. With the material in the proper position, using the hand wheel, lower the needle so that the first stitch falls close to the edge. Then lower the presser foot. Hold the two threads in back while making the first two stitches. This procedure prevents the threads from being tangled in the seam or in the bobbin case.

Until you are sure of your skill, stitch slowly. Guide the material with a light pressure of the fingers. The machine will control the fabric if you do not pull or push it.

Guiding. Put your fingers lightly on the material. The fingertips will be enough. Allow the right hand to guide the work and the left one to hold it in place. Sew at an even, steady pace. Starting and stopping make it difficult to stitch in a straight line.

Sometimes the fabric needs to be stretched slightly. To do this, put the fin-

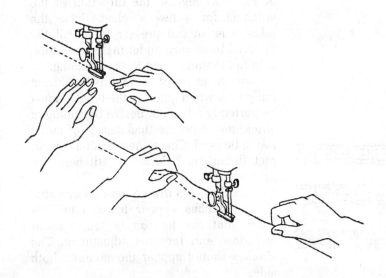

ger over the edge of the fabric and pull gently. Keep the right hand in front, the left hand in back.

Ending. There are two ways to fasten the ends of the threads. It can be done by tying or by back-tacking. To tie the threads, stop the machine at the end of the row so the last stitch falls at the edge of the material. To release the tension, raise the take-up lever to its highest point. Also raise the presser foot. Pull the material to the back so the threads can be cut. Be sure that enough thread is left on the machine so it will not become unthreaded the next time it is used. In order to tie the threads together, jerk one thread so the other thread can be pulled through the fabric. When both threads are together, tie them together securely and close to the material. Clip the ends.

To use the back-tack method at the end of the row, reverse the direction of the stitching for a few stitches. Raise the take-up lever and presser foot. Pull the material backward under the presser foot. Clip the threads close to the stitching.

Tension. In order to obtain the correct puffy look when quilting, the tension must be perfectly adjusted. Before beginning to stitch, test it on the thicknesses of material to be used. Check the machine for correct threading, balance of stitches, and pressure.

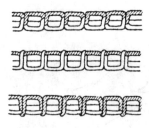

If the thread is drawn tight on one side or the stitches appear loose, then you know that the tension is too tight or too loose and requires adjustment. The stitches should appear the same on both sides.

Pressure. It is important that the fabric be held in place between the presser foot and the feed dog with the correct amount of pressure. If the two edges of material match at the end of the stitching, then you know the pressure is correct. If the upper layer, however, extends beyond the lower edge, then you know the pressure is too heavy. If the fabric does not move along at an even pace, then the pressure may be too tight. For quilting through the thickness of the three layers an adjustment may be required.

Sewing Procedures

The construction and finishing of a quilted article require a knowledge of certain basic sewing techniques. For instance, seams must be made, edges finished, and decorative touches added. Some suggestions for doing just that are given here.

SEAMING

Although there are many types of seams, the plain seam is the one you will use most often for your quilting projects. It is the easiest one to make and works nicely on straight and curved seams.

Plain Seam. Start by pinning two pieces of material together, usually the right sides. The edges should be evenly placed and the ends matching. Insert the pins at right angles to the seam line. Be sure the pins hold the two pieces together firmly. If you

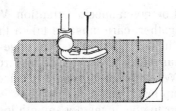

do not feel that you have perfect control of the machine, then it may be best to baste the edges together, removing the pins as you sew. The two pieces can be sewn together by hand or machine. If you prefer hand sewing, use a row of backstitches for a strong seam. If you prefer machine stitches, however, be sure that you sew for perfection.

For a stitched seam, begin by placing the article carefully under the presser foot so that the first stitch will fall at the edge of the material. It is better to stitch slowly, removing each pin with your right hand just before the machine foot reaches it. Guide the cloth lightly with your fingertips. Stop stitching at the edge of the fabric so the last stitch is made in it. A seam guide will help keep the stitching straight. Although the stitches are usually secured at the ends of a row of stitches by tying or back-tacking, it usually isn't necessary when quilting because the stitching line will be secured by another.

Curved seams are more difficult to make than straight ones. Using small stitches and stitching slowly will make it easier to produce a perfect curve. In order to make the seam lie flat, it must be clipped or notched. For an inward curve, clip almost to the seam line about every 1/4 inch (6 mm). On an outward curve, cut notches almost to the line of stitching.

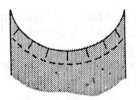 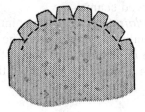

Bias edges must be given special attention. When the edges are being sewn together, care must be taken that the seam is not stretched or puckered. When a bias edge is sewed to a straight one, the bias edge should be held toward you, on top of the straight one. When fullness must be "eased" into place, hold the full side up or toward you.

Pressing. In order to give a seam a smooth look, it should be pressed first on one side and then on the other. Although a seam is usually pressed open, in quilt-making procedures it is often pressed to one side. When seaming patchwork pieces together, quilters feel that a seam pressed to the side is stronger.

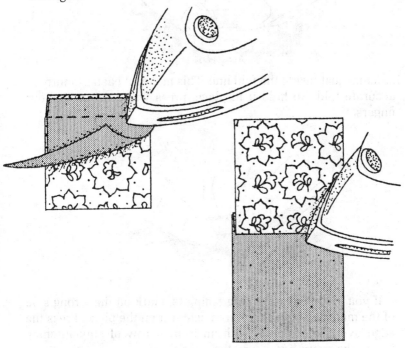

EDGE FINISHES

Raw edges can be finished in various ways. The edges can just be turned under or they can be finished with a hem, a binding, a facing, and certain stitches. The treatment depends on the item and the effect desired.

Turning Edges. There are certain quilting procedures such as appliqué that require the raw edges to be turned under. This must be done with great care. In some instances, the creasing can be done by finger pressing. Fold the fabric on the seam—or hemline—and press the edge firmly with the fingers. If the crease line does not seem to hold, try pressing with the tip of an iron. Be careful not to stretch the fabric.

If you find it difficult to fold the material, put a row of stay-

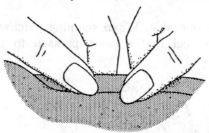

stitching just inside the fold line. This makes it easier to turn an accurate fold. To hold it in place, press with an iron or your fingers.

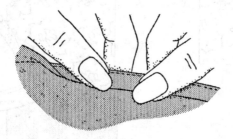

If you are using a marking template, mark on the wrong side of the material, being careful to center it on the piece. Press the edge over the template with an iron. A row of stay-stitching inside the seam line keeps the edge even.

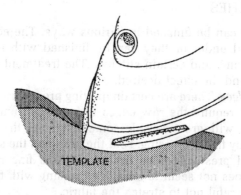

TEMPLATE

Curved Edges. It is important that curved edges lie flat. To ensure this, the edges must be clipped or notched. A row of stay-stitching inside the seam line will help control the length of the clips and notches.

For an inward or concave curve, clip the edge almost to the stay-stitching at intervals of 1/4 inch (6 mm). Use the points of sharp scissors.

For an outward or convex curve, cut notches almost to the stay-stitched line. Make notches about every 1/4 inch (6 mm) apart.

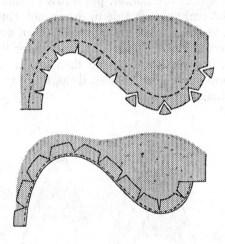

Cornered Edges. Turning corners is one of the more difficult sewing processes to do, and it is most important that it be done with precision.

For an inward corner, place a row of stay-stitches at least 1 inch (2.5 cm) on each side of a corner. Run a pin diagonally through the stitches at the corner. This will keep you from cutting the stitches when you clip the fabric. Clip into the corner

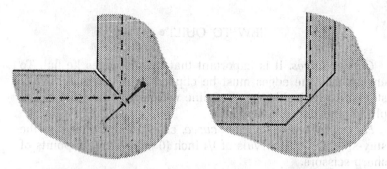

almost to the stitching line. When you turn the edges under, you will notice that a diagonal has been formed and the corner lies flat.

For a point or outward corner, put a row of stay-stitches at least 1 inch (2.5 cm) on each side of the corner. Cut off half of the seam allowance, across the point (A). Turn under the remaining portion across the point (B). Fold under the seam allowances (C), first on one side and then on the other, being sure that a good sharp point results. If there is any excess material protruding, trim it off (D).

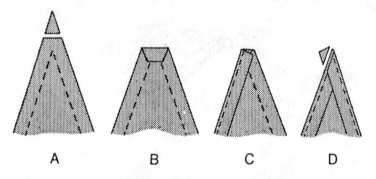

A   B   C   D

Hems. A hem not only finishes a raw edge but also maintains the shape of an article. Hems can be made in a variety of widths depending on where they are to be used.

For a narrow machine-stitched hem, place a row of machine stitches 1/8 inch (3 mm) from the raw edge. This stays the edge and acts as a guide. Fold under the raw edge on the line of stitching. Pressing it with the fingertips makes the stitching easier. Then turn the folded edge under the same width and finger-press. Baste if you feel the fabric needs more controlling. Stitch in place.

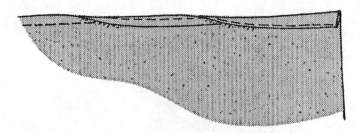

For a narrow hand-sewn hem, turn under the edge ⅛ inch (3 mm) and stitch close to it. Fold under the folded edge the same width and sew it in place with a hemming stitch. You may want to baste the hem in place before sewing it in order to keep the width of the hem even.

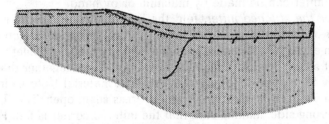

For a wider hem, use the same procedure. The only difference is in the width of the second fold. It is possible to stitch this type of hem by machine as well as by hand.

A graded hem is sometimes used to finish the edge of a quilt. The top and inner layers are trimmed to the desired size. Then the lower layer is folded over the top and the batting, covering the edges. The edge of the underlayer is folded under and

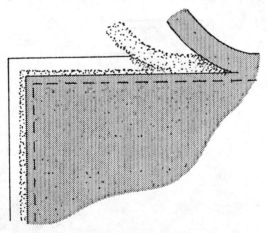

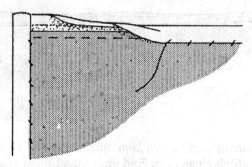

basted to the top and then slip-stitched into place. It produces a finish similar in appearance to a bound edge.

Hem with a *mitered corner,* which produces a nice finish. The miter can be made by machine or by hand.

For the stitched miter, fold the hem allowance to the right side of the article you are making. Fold the miter diagonally from edge point to inner spot where edges of the hem meet with right sides together. Stitch the hem allowances together diagonally from point to inner edge (A). Trim material 1/4 to 1/2 inch (3 to 6 mm) from stitching line (B). Press seam open. Turn hem to wrong side, making sure that the mitered corner is flat. Fold under the raw edge of the hem and sew in place (C).

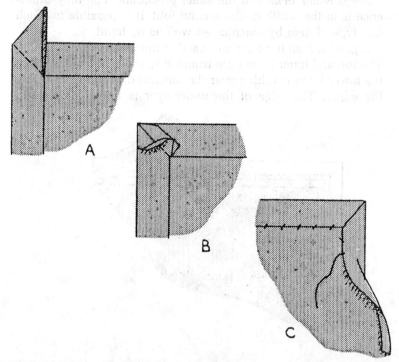

A

B

C

For a hand-finished miter, fold hem to wrong side. Form miter at corner from outer point diagonally to edge of hem. This forms a diagonal line across the point. Place material flat and open. Cut ¼ inch (3 mm) off corner on diagonal line. Also fold under the raw edges of hem ¼ inch (3 mm). Turn hem to wrong side. Bring folded diagonal edges together. Using tiny whipping stitches, sew edges of miter together.

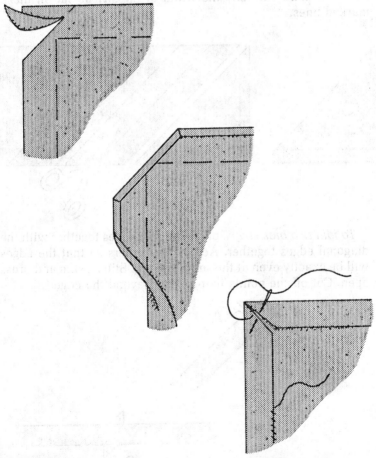

Bound Edges. Although binding is employed to finish and strengthen a raw edge, it can also add a decorative touch. It is made of a bias strip that you can make or purchase.

To cut a bias strip, straighten the material on both the length-wise and crosswise grains. Fold the fabric so that the length-wise and crosswise threads are parallel to each other, making a diagonal fold that is the true bias. In using bias, it is impor-tant that it be a true bias. Cut the material on the diagonal fold.

The width of the bias strip you cut depends on the desired width of the finished width plus two seam allowances. Mea-sure and mark carefully the width of the strips. Cut on these marked lines.

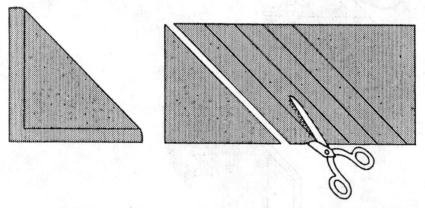

To join two bias strips, place the right sides together with the diagonal edges together. Adjust the corners so that the edges will be exactly even at the seam line (A). Stitch seam and press open. Cut off the points that extend beyond the edge (B).

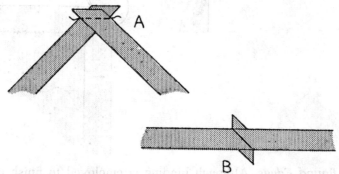

To attach the bias binding, pin strip to the right side of the item so the center of the binding will fold over edge. If you are

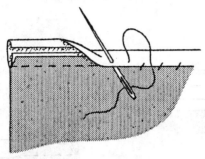

working on a curved edge, stretch the strip on an inside curve and ease it on an outside one. Stitch binding at seam line. Bring binding over the edge to the wrong side. Fold under the raw edge of the binding. Hem along stitching line.

Sometimes the finishing is done on the right side. To do this, the binding is first stitched to the wrong side and then brought to the right side for finishing. Generally it is held in place with topstitching.

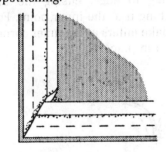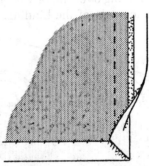

To bind an outward corner, sew the binding to the point. Before turning the corner, make sure that there is enough at the corner in order to miter it. Continue stitching. Be careful not to catch in the stitching the fold that is allowed for the miter. Turn bias to inside. At the corner, turn the binding over the edge, forming a miter to the point on both sides of the binding. Turn the edge under and hem in place.

To bind an inward corner, stitch the binding to the edge, pulling it tight at the corner. Leave the needle in the material at the corner. Raise the presser foot and pivot the material to turn

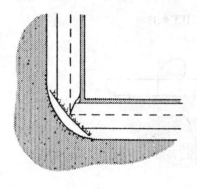

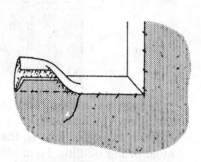

the corner and then continue stitching. Turn binding to wrong side. Turn a miter fold in place by slip-stitching. Turn in raw edge of binding. Hem in place on wrong side of article.

To bind scallops, sew binding to edge, easing the bias around the full curve and stretching it at the inner point. Fold the binding over the raw edge. Make miters at the inner corners on each side of the binding. Hem in place.

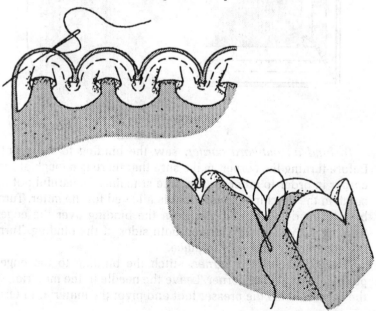

6

The Basics of Quilting

The basic quilting technique, as I've said, uses easy-to-make running stitches to hold securely a soft filler between two layers of material. Not only do the stitches give the surface a design interest with all-over textured effect, but they also add strength to the material.

Whether to do the quilting by hand or machine is a decision that has to be made. It all depends on the effect you wish, how experienced a sewer you are, and how much time you have to make the project. If it is an heirloom item you want to make, you should do it by hand. If the article, however, falls into the utilitarian category, then machine stitches will be more practical.

Hand quilting can be tedious. It is slow work and must be done with precision. It is possible, however, to feel joy when you watch beautiful little stitches appear. With this feeling and practice, you can develop a rhythm that helps you to work more quickly.

Although quilting is usually associated with quilt making, it can be employed in many other ways. Home fashions, such as wall hangings, pillows, and place mats, as well as personal fashions, such as jackets, vests, and skirts, may be given a distinctive touch by the addition of a quilted detail.

Types of Design

Variations in designs for quilting are many. They range from
the simple straight lines to graceful curves found in feathers
and butterflies. There are no specific rules to guide you in your
selection. It all depends on your artistic sense and ability to
choose an appropriate design for the article you are creating.

Before making your decision, it is a good idea to study the
quilting designs of old quilts. You often find there a great deal
of originality and artistic expression. They also show you how
quilting stitches can be coordinated with patchwork and appliqué designs. Sometimes an ornamental motif can be used to
decorate a plain block when the quilt is made of alternating
patchwork or appliqué blocks.

ALL-OVER DESIGNS

The consistent repetition of one or more lines and shapes,
producing a regular pattern, is the dominating characteristic of
this type of quilting. The designs can be simple or complicated
and can be adapted for spaces of any size. It is possible to use
them to decorate a total area, as for a whole-cloth quilt and a
plain block, or to give interest to a smaller area.

Some of the all-over patterns are not especially interesting,
but they have been used for a long time. They do their job well,
holding the layers together and at the same time giving the
material a decorative surface.

Straight-Line Designs. These are probably the most frequently used patterns. They are easy to quilt, both by hand and
by machine. Vertical or horizontal lines, drawn parallel to each
other, produce a tunnel effect; diagonal lines, a zigzag one.

Another way to use these lines is to cross the lines, creating
a series of squares or diamonds. The crisscrossed designs are
often used to surround a quilted motif, giving it more prominence. After you have decided on the design and size, you can
draw the guidelines on the fabric, using a pencil and ruler.

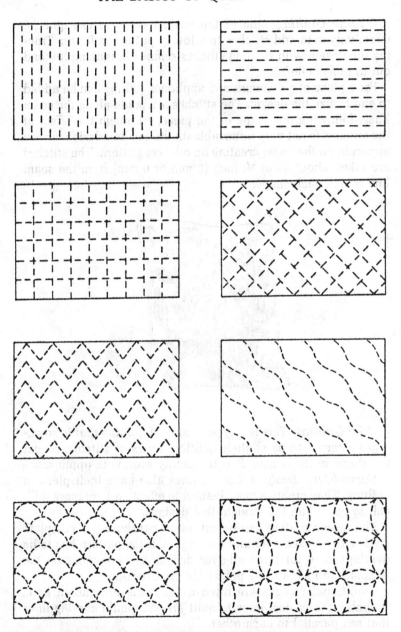

Outline Quilting. One of the easiest ways to use quilting effectively is to add stitches to a lovely patterned fabric. Tracing the design with running stitches defines it, making it stand out in puffy relief.

For a piece of patchwork and appliqué, quilting can be added to emphasize the design. The stitches are made along the seam lines, following the shape of the piece. Although the effect of the stitches is not very noticeable on the top, the design is very apparent on the back, creating an all-over pattern. The stitches are taken about 1/8 or 1/4 inch (3 mm or 6 mm) from the seam line within each shape.

Echo Quilting. This is a type of outline quilting that is sometimes referred to as contour quilting. Rows of stitches repeat the shape of the design. It is frequently seen with appliqués.

Curved-Line Designs. Curved lines also have their place in quilting. They create a more elaborate effect and are more difficult to quilt than the straight-line designs.

The design pattern can be cut out of cardboard. A complete circle can be used over and over again. If the pattern has to be overlapped to form the all-over design, mark notches on the template to indicate the points for the overlap.

Traditional designs are often used. Some are shown here. Probably the easiest ones to quilt are the gentle curving lines that run parallel to each other.

For the shell pattern, the same shape is repeated row upon row. However, its position is changed in alternating rows. Although the design is the same, the pattern must be carefully placed and with precision.

Overlapping circles create a flowerlike motif. It is hard to detect how the design is made. A circle is all you need for the pattern. Mark the round template to indicate the places on the circle where the overlapping will take place.

Scallops or crescents appear when two circles of different sizes work together. In determining the shape of the design, the smaller circle shapes the upper curve, and the larger circle shapes the lower one. Be sure to mark the top and bottom of the curves on the template and the joining points.

DECORATIVE MOTIFS

To give a more elaborate look to the quilting, an ornamental motif is made part of the all-over design. Often it becomes the center of interest with a simple all-over design acting as the background or filler for the plain area surrounding the motif.

The decorative designs frequently seem to be still lifes of traditional subjects such as fruits, flowers, and baskets. Often there is a formality about this type of design. Some contain complicated details that require a plain fabric background to show off their beauty because the design would be lost on printed material. Sometimes smaller versions of the central motif are placed about it or in the corners for a lovely effect.

Planning the Design. This requires a great deal of thought. The over-all effect should create a coordinated picture. Working out the design on graph paper is a good way to achieve this effect. Be sure to think of it in relation to the place where it is to be used.

Patterns for these decorative designs can be purchased or you can design your own. For the quilting, use tiny stitches: they make it possible for you to define the intricate details, especially the tight curves that seem to be so much a part of these designs.

BORDER DESIGNS

Another area that provides a place for quilting is the border. It acts as a frame, providing a lovely finish to the central design whether it be patchwork, appliqué, or just quilting. As a frame, it should complement the main design and relate to the general theme. If you study old quilts, you will notice that the designs seem to have intertwined motifs with wavelike curves and graceful feathers flowing along the edge. Today many of the borders are more geometric in feeling, with all-over designs used effectively.

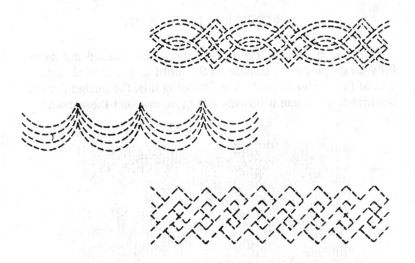

Around the Corner. The design can flow smoothly around the corner or a decorative motif can be introduced with the border balanced on each side of it. Sometimes the border design can be adapted to fit the corner in one continuous line, and at others, a new but related design detail can be added. Another way to handle the corners is to introduce a decorative block, using a different but related motif. This works nicely when the border design remains balanced on each side.

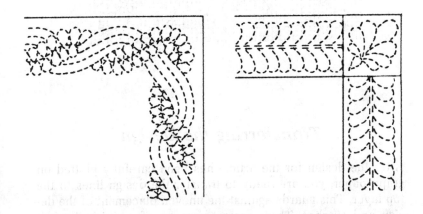

Planning a Border. The design should be worked out carefully on graph paper. Decide on the motif to use in each corner and at the center of each side. By doing this, the design is kept balanced. Then use a flowing design to connect these points.

Transferring the Design

After the design for the article has been carefully plotted on graph paper, you are ready to transfer the design lines to the top layer. This guards against the uneven placement of the design and stitches. There are many ways of marking. Experiment with some of them so that you know which one is the easiest for you to use.

MARKING THE TOP LAYER

When to Do It. Transferring the design can be done before or after the top layer is basted to the batting and bottom layer. It also can be done before or after it is mounted in the frame or hoop. It has always seemed easier to do it when the top is still in its single state. There is a softness to the material that makes it difficult to control the accuracy of the lines if the marking is done after the batting is in place.

If you decide to assemble the three layers and put them in the frame before marking, you will find it best to mark only a small section at a time. Quilt this before marking another section. In this way, you will avoid smudging the lines.

Pencil Marking. Probably the method employed most often to mark a design is to use a number 2 pencil or an artist's chalk pencil directly on the fabric. The pencil should be well sharpened in order to draw lightly along the ruler, template, or stencil. You just want a fine line that is barely visible and may be removed by washing. Be sure to avoid a heavy line.

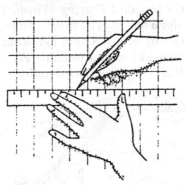

Perforated Pattern. This method works well when marking nongeometric designs for plain blocks and whole-cloth quilts. It is possible to buy perforated patterns for many of the traditional designs. However, if you prefer to create your own design, you can perforate it by using an unthreaded sewing

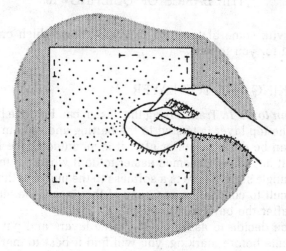

machine needle or a fine nail. Rubbing lightly with a fine sand-paper on the underside will open the holes.

With the pattern pinned in place, use a soft cloth or cotton ball over the holes to dust cinnamon when working on light colors, cornstarch or French chalk on dark colors. Then lift the pattern carefully. Draw over the design lightly with a pencil. Gently brush or shake the powder off the fabric when the marking has been completed.

Dressmaker's Carbon and Tracing Wheel. These offer an-other way to transfer a design. The tracing wheel that produces a dotted line is the one to use. Use a light-colored carbon. Be sure it will leave no marking after washing. As you trace, check the transfer by lifting the paper occasionally.

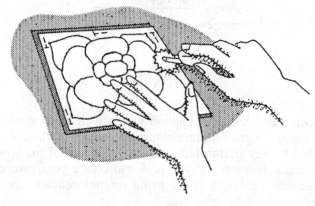

Pin a line-drawing pattern to the right side of the fabric. Slip the carbon, in an appropriate color, under the pattern with the carbon side down. Follow the lines carefully with the tracing wheel.

Mylar and Tracing Wheel. The tracing wheel does have a tendency to tear the paper. To avoid this, a more durable pattern of Mylar, which is a paper-thin plastic, can be used. Draw the pattern on the plastic and proceed as if you were using a paper pattern.

Layering the Materials

Preparation of the material to be quilted is most important. Unless it is carefully done, the finished product will not be perfect.

Begin by pressing the material, no matter what the size is, with the grain so it will be smooth and without a wrinkle.

ARRANGING THE LAYERS

As I have already mentioned, quilting is made of three layers of material. A layer of batting is sandwiched between an upper and a lower layer of fabric.

Begin with the Backing. Place the bottom layer, wrong side up, on a flat surface. If it is a large piece, the floor may be the best place to work. Sometimes it is necessary to sew several widths of cloth together in order to obtain the required size. When you do this, be sure the seams are up when the piece is laid out.

Smooth out the fabric so it is perfectly flat. Work from the center to the edges, making sure to keep the material in perfect alignment. Anchoring the corners with thumbtacks will hold it in place.

Add the Batting. On top of the backing, place a layer of batting. Unroll it carefully so you won't pull the backing out of place. Smooth it out evenly so there are no thick or thin places. The thickness of the batting should remain uniform throughout. Some quilters like to anchor the batting to the backing with

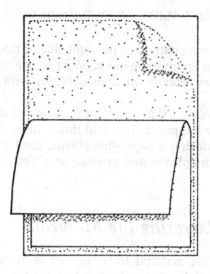

basting stitches, starting at the center and working toward the corners.

Put On the Top. Be sure the right side of the top layer is up. Work carefully so the edges are together unless the directions for the article you are making say otherwise. Starting at the center, smooth the top gently, working out any unevenness.

BASTING THE LAYERS

The three layers are held together with basting stitches. Although the basting is temporary, it should be made with great care so the layers remain unwrinkled and securely together throughout the quilting.

For the basting, use a single thread with a knot at the end. The stitches can be rather long, about 3 inches (7.5 cm). Since you will be basting with no guidelines, try to keep the lines as straight as possible. As you baste, let the hand that is not controlling the needle smooth out the layers, easing out any unevenness.

The amount of quilting you will be doing will influence the amount of basting you will need to keep the layers in place. The more you are going to handle the work, the more securely the layers must be held in place. This increases the amount of basting. If you are not using a frame or hoop, you will also need more rows of basting.

Direction of the Stitches. The lines the basting makes can vary in direction. Some quilters like to have the lines form a sunburst effect, others prefer a modified sunburst coupled with a series of vertical and horizontal lines, and still others prefer a type of diagonal basting that they call quilt basting. Try each and decide which one works best for you and the piece you are working on. You may find one way works better for a large piece than for a small piece.

For the sunburst effect, start at the center of the work and baste to each of the four corners, always beginning at the same point. Then, starting again at the center, baste to a point at the middle of each side. For a large piece, add lines between the other lines so they are 6 inches (15 cm) apart around the edges.

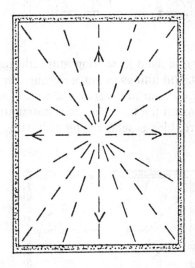

For a combination of lines, start with diagonal lines to the corners, always beginning at the center. Then add lines to the middle of each edge. Follow with rows of basting stitches placed parallel to the edges. Work outward from the center. Space the rows from 8 to 10 inches (20.5 cm to 25.5 cm) apart. The final row of stitches should be placed at the edge of the piece so that the batting will not slip away from the other two layers. See illustration on top of next page.

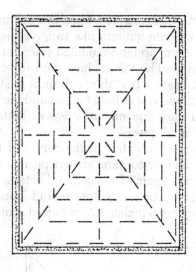

Diagonal basting is used in sewing and tailoring to hold interfacings, facings, and linings in place during fittings. For quilting, the stitches are taken in a vertical direction with a diagonal stitch appearing on the top side and a horizontal one on the underside. This provides a secure type of basting.

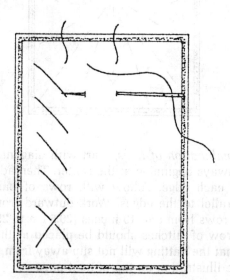

Start at the top of the layered piece with a knotted thread. Take a horizontal stitch on the underside, bringing the needle to the upper side. Continue to make these stitches, keeping them evenly spaced, to the lower edge. You can end the row of stitches by crossing the last one. Continue to work this way until the complete area is covered. Keep the rows about 2 inches (5 cm) apart.

Quilting by Hand

Since stitches create the design in all-over quilting, it is important that each one be made with great care. To ensure perfect results, the technique for making the stitch, using the right tools and supplies, must be mastered.

EQUIPMENT TO USE

Although it is generally felt that a more beautiful effect is produced when the layers of material are held taut in a large hoop or frame, it is possible to quilt without either. Working without a hoop is becoming popular for quilting small pieces. You can decide which way you prefer to work.

The Hoop. Select a round one about 23 inches (58.5 cm) in diameter. This is a convenient size to use. It does not occupy too much space and can be moved easily. Since it is best to have both hands free to quilt, it is better if the hoop sits in its own stand. If you do not have a stand, you can prop it against a table or some other appropriate piece of furniture.

When placing the basted material into the hoop, be sure to put it over the inner hoop, centering the design. Pull the material evenly and gently in all directions after putting on the top rim. Tighten the bolt if necessary to eliminate any possibility of the design becoming distorted. By keeping the material taut as you quilt, the possibility of producing wrinkles on the underside of the work is avoided. Also this helps to create a puffy effect between the rows of stitches when the hoop is removed, releasing the tension on the materials. The amount of puffiness

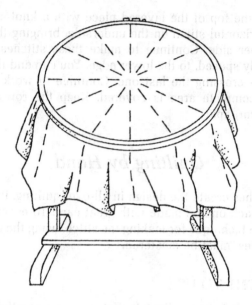

will depend to some extent on the type of batting you are using. There will not be as much with cotton batting as with the synthetic type.

When the quilting in the center area is completed, remove the hoop. Reposition the material so you can quilt another area. Always quilt outward toward the edge, but be sure to do it evenly. See top of page 113.

The hoop can also be used when quilting outer edges, such as borders and corners. To do this, it is necessary to extend the area to be quilted with muslin strips so that it can be held taut by the hoop. The muslin strips can also be used for small projects, such as pillows that are too small to be stretched evenly in the hoop.

Strips about 6 to 8 inches (15 to 20.5 cm) wide are handy to use. They can be 30 inches (76 cm) or more in length. For a corner, you will need two muslin strips with ends butted together. If the project is small, then four strips are required.

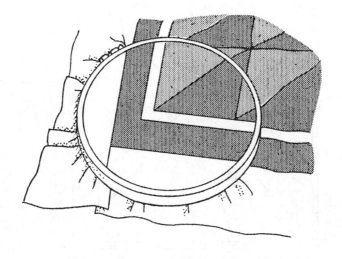

The Frame. If you have the space in your house, you may find the quilting frame more convenient to use for large projects such as a quilt. It is possible to keep the quilting in one position, thus eliminating constant moving.

The way in which the material is attached to the frame will depend to some extent on the type of frame you are using. However, in general, the method used is about the same as that with the hoop.

The bars or rails should have strips of material tacked or stapled to them. If they don't, cut two strips of sturdy fabric such as ticking. They should be 2 or 3 inches (5 or 7.5 cm) wide and as long as the bars on which the quilting will be rolled.

Fold each strip in half. Baste the long edges together. Mark the center points of the strips and the bars. Staple or tack each strip to a bar, keeping it an even distance from the edge.

To attach the project to the bars, lay it flat on the floor. Place a bar at each end, parallel to the material and with the center points of bar and project matching. Baste the layers to be quilted to the ticking strip, starting at the middle and sewing

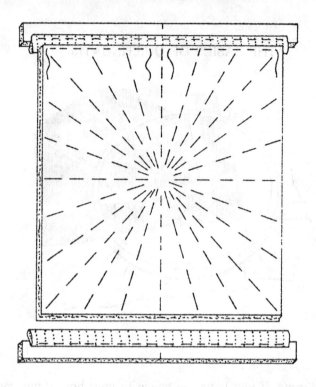

out to each edge. Baste carefully with heavy thread. It may be necessary to do this several times so that the material will hold securely when stretched tightly in the frame. Be sure to keep the ends in perfect alignment so that the quilting can be done with precision.

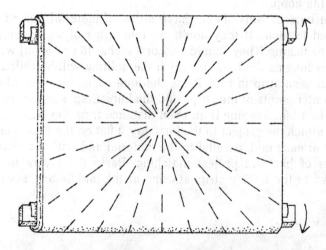

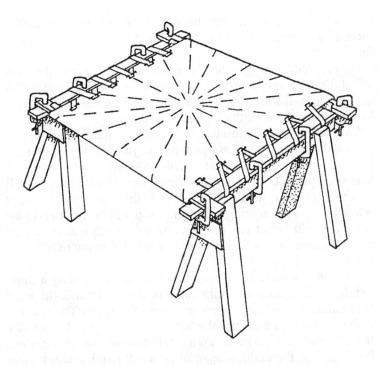

When both ends are attached, roll the materials evenly and tautly onto each bar, keeping the central area exposed for quilting. With the material in place, attach the bars. The way this is done will depend on the type of frame you are using.

The Needle. To begin the quilting, you need a needle that will allow you to take tiny, even stitches, penetrating the fabric layers easily. A number 8 between or quilting needle usually works well. It is short and narrow with a fine eye.

The Thread. Regular sewing thread as well as quilting thread can be used. It should be of medium weight; a number 40 or 50 works well. A cotton thread is usually best, especially if you are using cotton fabric. The special quilting thread has a glaze finish that seems to strengthen the thread and help to prevent knots. Regular thread can be strengthened by running it over a cake of beeswax. A single thread, no longer than 18 inches (46 cm), will help prevent the threads from tangling. A longer thread has a tendency to knot and break before the quilting is finished.

As for color, you can decide which one will create the best effect. Usually only one color is used when making a quilt with many colors. It should be chosen carefully so the color blends inconspicuously with the background color.

The Thimble. A thimble is a "must" for quilting. Although you may have avoided using a thimble, you will find it difficult to take tiny stitches without it. Not only will your stitches be less than perfect, but your fingers may be bloody and sore. If you feel you can never get used to a thimble, try wearing it when you are not sewing or quilting. You will be surprised how soon you will forget you are wearing it; it will seem to be part of your finger. If you finally decide a thimble is impossible, try taping your finger.

You really should have two thimbles. One is worn by a right-handed quilter on the middle finger of the right hand, the hand that makes the stitches working above the work. The other is worn on the first finger of the left hand, which works beneath the material. Of course, if you are left-handed, one thimble will be placed on the middle finger of your left hand, and the other thimble on the first finger of your right hand.

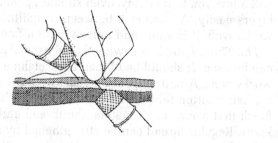

THE STITCH

A simple running stitch is used. However, the effect seems different than when it is used for sewing. The stitches should be very short, even, and closely spaced. This regularity seems to produce the illusion of an unbroken line. In fact the stitches seem less obvious than the indented effect they create on the surface of the material.

The Size. As for the size of the stitch, opinions differ. Very old quilts were made with minute stitches, sometimes 20 to the inch. This detail offers a way of appraising the age of a quilt. Today it seems almost impossible for quilters to make the tiny stitches of yesteryear. This may in part be due to the use of synthetic fabrics.

Some experienced quilters feel that the size of the stitch is not as important as the over-all look of uniformity in the stitches and spacing, creating a neat look. Others feel you should aim for 12 stitches per inch. However, the weight and thickness of the batting will determine to some extent how many stitches you can make to the inch. Usually 5 to 8 stitches on the top side produce attractive quilting.

– – – – – – – – – **16 stitches to the inch**

— — — — · **8 stitches to the inch**

Construction Detail. There are two ways to make the running stitch for quilting. You can make one stitch at a time or you can weave the needle in and out through all of the layers, taking two or three little stitches before drawing the needle and thread through the material. Before you decide which one to use, try both. Practice on a small piece. As you do this, you will develop a rhythmic movement that will help to keep your stitches the same size.

Beginning. Cut a length of thread no longer than 18 inches. A longer thread tends to tangle and may wear thin and break. As I've said, you may find waxing the thread with beeswax will prove helpful in avoiding these problems.

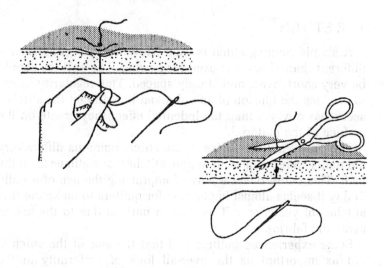

Place a small knot at one end of the single thread. Then, with your thimble in place, hold the needle with the thumb and first finger at about the middle point. Insert the needle so it penetrates first the top layer and then the other two. Push the needle through the layers with the thimbled finger. The eye of the needle should fit firmly into one of the indentations in the thimble.

Pull the thread through the layers. In order to conceal the knot, tug gently but firmly on the thread until the knot passes through the top layer and becomes embedded in the batting layer. If a thread end shows above the top layer, snip it off, but be careful not to cut the fabric.

Sewing Procedures. As the needle penetrates the material from the top, it encounters the finger below. To protect it, wear a thimble or cover it with a piece of tape. The hand beneath the material is held palm up so that the first finger, protected by a thimble, can come in contact with the needle. Push the edge of the lower thimble up against the backing gently so that a ridge is made on the upper side of the material just below the quilting line. Guide the needle from above into the ridge and against the lower thimble. Continue this motion, pushing the needle back up through the top a short distance away using the side of

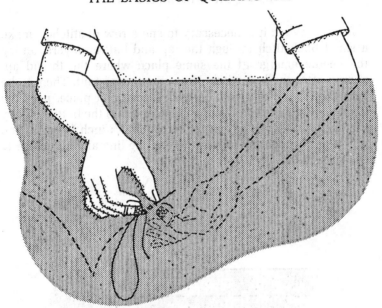

the upper thimble. Always be sure that the needle penetrates all three layers of fabric. During this process the thumb of the upper hand plays an important function. It seems to automatically press down on the quilting line of the material a short distance ahead of the point where the needle appears ready to begin the next stitch. The movement of the thumb seems to be a regulating force, helping to keep the spaces between the stitches tiny and uniform in length.

The lower thimble also provides a control over the spacing and size of the stitches if you always hold it in about the same position along the quilting line. If you feel the needle touching the thimble, you know that the needle has passed through the backing.

The thread seen on the surface of the quilting indicates the size of the stitch. At first you may have trouble gauging the size of each stitch, taking tentative steps before you actually make the next stitch. Gradually you will develop a feeling for the point where the needle should be inserted. The rhythm soon produces a sense of pleasure in your work.

Ending. When it is necessary to end a row of stitches, make a small backstitch through the top and batting layers, letting the needle emerge at the same place where the thread appeared after the last stitch. Draw the thread taut. Then, to be sure that the thread will be held securely in place, pass the needle and thread through the stitch and into the batting. Carry the needle through the batting for about 3/4 inch (2 cm). Then pull it up through the top on the quilting line and clip close to the surface.

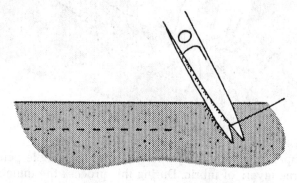

If at first this procedure seems tedious, don't be discouraged. After a little practice you will develop a natural rhythm. You will find great enjoyment in watching the needle run through the material and appear at specific intervals.

HELPFUL TIPS

As your quilting progresses, you will find yourself not only doing straight lines but also reproducing pictorial designs with curving ones. In order to avoid constantly turning your work, use these suggestions. They will make your work easier and faster to do.

Start and Direction. The point where you begin and the direction you follow influence the look of your work. Starting in the center of a design and quilting toward you will help to keep the material from puckering.

Whether quilting by hand or by machine, it is usually best to quilt outward from the middle of the piece, moving away from the completed area. Do not hop from one motif to another that is separated by an unquilted area unless the design has been planned that way.

Turning Corners. If the design requires the turning of corners, you will find it quicker to work with several needles. Do one row at a time, leaving the needle at the corner. After you have completed all the rows in this way, turn the work to its new position. Begin to quilt again, picking up each needle in a row to complete the row. If you are working on a frame, this method works nicely when a new area must be rolled into position in order for you to continue quilting.

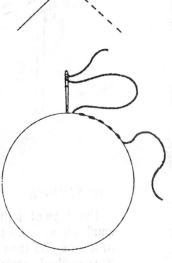

Circular or Curved Designs. In order always to quilt toward yourself, cut a double length of thread. Insert a threaded needle to the right of the starting point. As you make your first stitch, do not pull the thread completely through. Instead, leave half of the thread dangling. Continue to quilt to the left for a certain distance. Then pick up the dangling thread and continue to quilt, completing the design.

Lines Close Together. When you are quilting more complicated designs with the lines close together, try to avoid stopping and starting at each new line. Instead, carry the thread through the batting from the finished to the beginning spot. You can also follow this procedure when moving from one motif to another.

Without a Hoop or Frame. Quilting can be done without a hoop or frame. The finished work may not have as professional a look, but the quilted effect can be obtained.

For *small pieces,* work in your lap, spreading the project over it. A lap board on which to rest the layered material is helpful.

For *larger projects,* use a table or ironing board large enough to support the project's full weight. If you allow a large portion of the article to hang over the sides, the weight may pull it out of shape. Rolling or folding up the sides will help to eliminate this situation.

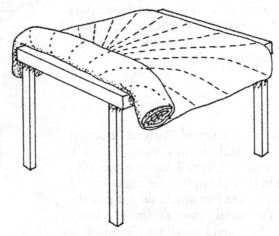

Unit Quilting

This type of quilting makes it simpler for you to work, since small pieces are easier to handle. You quilt one block or panel at a time and then assemble the parts to make a larger piece. This method works nicely when you are quilting by machine. And, of course, it makes the work easy to carry. The quilting can be done without a frame or hoop and so requires little space in which to quilt.

After the block or section for the top is prepared, cut the backing and filler, keeping in mind that the top and bottom layers are cut the same size, but the seam allowances are removed from the filling layer, making it smaller.

Mark the quilting design on the top layer and then assemble the three layers. Baste them together carefully.

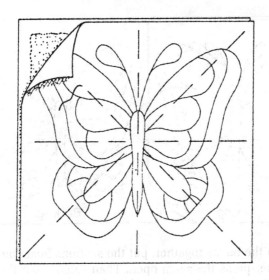

As you quilt the design, remember to leave the seam allowance free. This is necessary so that the parts can be joined.

When all of the sections have been made, sew the adjoining sections together. Place the right sides of the tops together after the basting stitches have been removed. Remember, only the tops are seamed together. This can be done by hand or machine, but be sure that the seam is straight and even.

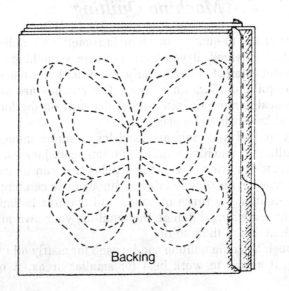

Backing

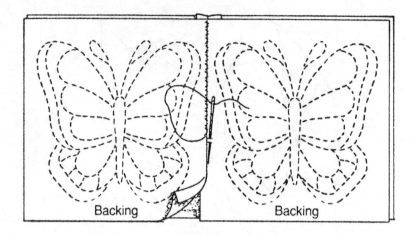

Backing   Backing

To seam the backs together, put the sections face down on a table. Finger-press the seam open. Then smooth out the edges of the batting so they just meet. If the batting overlaps, trim off the extra amount.

Fold under the seam allowance along one edge. Place it over the other section. Slip-stitch the folded edge in place, using small stitches to hold it securely.

Machine Quilting

Whether or not to quilt by machine is something a quilter has to decide for herself. If you want to make something quickly and are not interested particularly in an heirloom piece, then machine quilting offers an answer. The stitches are stronger and the design more definite. It just depends on the look you want and how it is to be used.

Today quilted materials are used for so many things other than quilts that machine quilting is often seen. Jackets, robes, and accessories are a few of the articles that can be made of various types of decorative fabric. Although you can buy fabric already quilted, the range of colors and textures is limited. If you want something different, then quilting your own material by machine is the thing to do.

Although machine quilting can be used for nearly all types of quilting, it seems to work best for smaller areas. A quilt is difficult to handle on a machine. Maneuvering the material under the arm of the machine is often tricky. Working in blocks or narrow sections will be easier.

HANDLING DESIGN DETAILS

Select your quilting design carefully. Curved lines and intricate patterns, which require many turnings, are just too awkward to do. Straight-line designs, extending from one edge to another, are easier and quicker to do.

Sewing Details. The three layers to be quilted should be carefully and securely basted together. It is important that the layers do not shift when being stitched.

Adjust the machine, loosening the tension and decreasing the pressure if necessary to eliminate any possibility of puckering or layers riding apart while stitching. Regulate the stitch length so there are about 10 to 12 stitches per inch (2.5 cm). Be sure to test these adjustments by stitching on a sample of the three layers you are using.

If you are stitching a grid design, you will find it much quicker and easier to keep the lines accurate if you use a quilter. This is a sewing machine attachment made especially to simplify the sewing process.

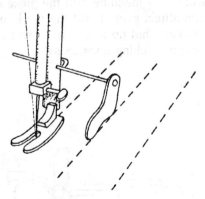

Fasten the quilter to the machine. The guiding prong can be turned in the holder, which makes it possible to regulate the placement of the guide so that it does not rest too heavily on the material. The guide can also be shifted back and forth in the holder. This allows you to make the rows of stitching the desired distance apart.

Be sure to consider the direction and sequence of the stitching lines before you begin to stitch. Try always to keep the bulk of the work to the left of the needle whenever possible. In order to prevent a pull on the material, place a table close to the machine on which a large piece, such as a quilt, can be supported.

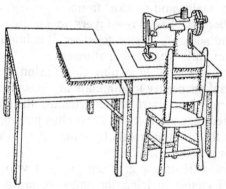

If the project you are working on seems difficult to handle under the arm of the machine, roll the piece up so it fits more easily. As you stitch, smooth out the work as it passes under the needle. Be sure that no tucks are sewn into the material at points where the stitching lines cross.

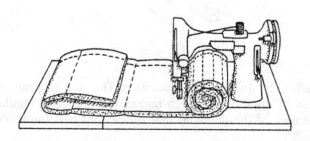

Begin the stitching in the middle of the project, working toward the outer edges as the quilting progresses. This keeps the layers from shifting and puckering.

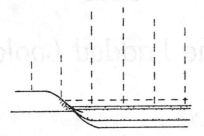

It is not necessary to fasten the beginning and ending threads at the edges. The edge finish, such as a binding, will secure the threads. However, if the stitching begins and ends some distance from the raw edges, leave long thread ends on both top and bottom when removing the material. To fasten the threads, thread a needle with each one. Run the top needle through the filling for a short distance. Bring it to the surface, clipping the thread close to the quilted surface. Repeat for the lower thread and needle.

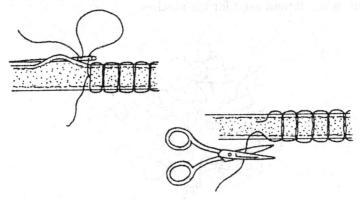

When you are stitching curved lines or around corners, you will have to raise the presser foot occasionally. This allows you to stitch smoothly around the curves and corners.

7

The Padded Look

As in most needlework, quilters keep trying to create something more and more beautiful. Not satisfied with just decorating a piece of plain fabric with little stitches, some women began experimenting. Certain parts of the quilted design were stuffed, creating a sculptured look with highlights and shadows. The effect was so lovely that it became a popular type of quilting in the eighteenth century. At first it was known as "white work." A whole-cloth quilt was made of white fabric with white thread used for the stitches.

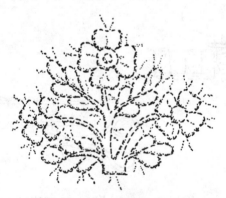

Trapunto Quilting

Today this type of quilting is called trapunto. Italy was probably its birthplace. After traveling to England about the time of

Queen Anne, it came to the American colonies, where it was especially popular in the South.

Although trapunto is a type of quilting, there is a difference in the construction of the quilted material. No batting is used for the middle layer. Instead the filler is made of a loosely woven material through which the stuffing can be passed and held in place. It is through these two layers of material that the quilting stitches are made. After the quilting is completed, the backing is sewn in place.

If you have a chance to inspect examples of early trapunto work, you will notice how fine the fabric is and how delicate the stitches. Unless the stitches were tiny, the elaborate design patterns did not stand out in bold relief. Baskets of flowers, vines, and leaves as well as feathery wreaths, prince's plumes, and cornucopias were the decorative designs frequently made. The motifs were scattered over the piece with diagonal lines, moving parallel to each other, filling in the areas between the designs and forming a nice background.

Today modern trapunto work is sometimes referred to as padded quilting. The designs are not quite so elaborate as formerly, but the construction is very much the same. Since trapunto work can be time-consuming, it is frequently used for just a small decorative touch, perhaps on an evening bag, a robe, a pillow. Another way to create trapunto quickly is to select a lovely printed fabric with a distinct motif. Be sure it has the small curved areas that can be outlined and stuffed easily.

THE MATERIALS

Trapunto quilting requires three layers of material—the regular top and bottom layers, but instead of a layer of batting there is a special interlining.

The Interlining. It should be made of a lightweight, loosely woven material. It controls the stuffing, holding it in the proper places to produce the three-dimensional effect. A good-quality cheesecloth, voile, or lightweight muslin can be used.

The Top Layer. The material for the top should be more

firmly woven. The choices are many, varying from plain broadcloth to shiny satin or sateen. Sometimes crisp fabrics such as chintz and taffeta are used. Although plain colors are usually employed, there are times when printed materials can be used most effectively. Try to find one with a well-defined motif that has areas that lend themselves to stuffing.

The Bottom Layer. It should be of the same type of material as the top when used for a quilt or similar article. The backing has to conceal the interlining and the openings for the stuffing. Be sure that whatever you choose has the body to make a good protective cover.

The Stuffing. The batting you use for quilting can be used for trapunto work. Instead of using it in large sheets, you should pull small pieces from the batt and tuck them into a specific section.

The Thread. It can be a regular cotton or synthetic thread used for other types of quilting. In order to give the padding prominence in the design, it is best to use a matching thread. Sometimes, for a special effect, you may want to try a silk twist.

TRANSFERRING THE DESIGN

Be sure to plan the layout for the entire design before beginning to transfer it to the material. Know exactly which parts are to be stuffed. Make certain that the design areas are bounded by stitches so the batting can be contained.

As for transferring the design, there are two ways of doing it. You can decide which way will work best for you. Ask yourself whether you want to quilt from the back or front. Can you make stitches that look as nice on the underside of the work as on the top? This is not always easy to do.

Working on the Underside. Transfer the design to the lightweight interlining. This can be done by tracing with a pencil. You will have a firm line to follow. However, there is one thing that you must watch carefully. The design was planned for the top side and, since you are working on the underside, the design must be reversed, tracing the mirror image if there is a definite right- and left-hand side to the design.

A beautiful example of appliqué work in which fabrics of various textures —cotton, wool, silk, and velvet—are mounted on muslin to create this Bird of Paradise design, a favorite one for a bride's quilt. It was made in Pough- keepsie, New York, in about 1860. Courtesy of Museum of American Folk Art

A dramatic effect is obtained when strips of fabric are used for piecing. In this case hand-dyed homespun was sewn and embroidered for the Kansas Baby pattern with a centered star adding a dramatic touch to the patriotic theme. The quilt was created in about 1861 in Kansas. Courtesy of Museum of American Folk Art

Hundreds of triangles were sewn together by Mrs. Raber of Indiana in about 1930 to create this dynamic pattern known as Ocean Waves (right). *Working with cotton in a variety of lights and darks, this Amish quilt was given a kaleidoscopic effect and was made by hand.* Courtesy of Museum of American Folk Art

About 1830 an unknown New England artist created this lovely design for stenciling. Scattering bouquets of flowers and stars over the top produces a pretty, delicate effect. Notice how the motifs are arranged to indicate the top and bottom of the spread. Courtesy of Museum of American Folk Art

A variety of techniques were used in about 1850 to create this lovely design known as Strawberries in Pots. Piecing, appliquéing, and trapunto played a role in the creation of this dramatic quilt. It was made in Missouri. Courtesy of Museum of American Folk Art

Appliquéd and embroidered cotton and silk were used for this summer spread. Each block bears a different design, often employed as a means to record one's favorite patterns. This album quilt was made in about 1860 in New York State. Courtesy of Museum of American Folk Art

Neckties provided Rosalind Ward with the inspiration and material for this original design. The close-up view shows the strip quilting technique used to blend the various colors, textures and patterns into a harmonious chevron design. Courtesy of Fairfield Processing Corporation

This entirely hand-pieced quilt (left) was made in western New York of bits of material from a ragbag. By outlining the blocks in a "garden maze" of bands, the quilt is given a certain unity although made from a variety of fabrics. Photo by Dan Babcock

A glorious example of the Star of Bethlehem pattern (below), made in the latter part of the nineteenth century in western New York. Smaller stars radiate from the center motif, giving a sunburst effect. In the collection of Eugenie Rives. Photo by Dan Babcock

The star (above) becomes more decorative when outlined with a feathered edge. One of the oldest pieced patterns, it is thought to be inspired by ancient mosaics. Setting the blocks together with a striped band and checkerboard corners gives an added importance to the top. The quilt was made in western New York in about 1860 and is in the collection of Eugenie P. Rives. Photo by Dan Babcock

Variations in color combinations and in the framing of the blocks show how the same block design can create different looks. The Basket of Lilies, also referred to as the Basket of Tulips, is one of the most charming of the old patchwork patterns. These quilts were made in Georgia in 1910. Photo by Dorothy and John Hill

Working on the Top Side. This requires very careful marking. The line must be very delicate, almost invisible, so that it
will not show after the stitches are made. A perforated pattern
dusted lightly with pounce is one way. Pricking the pattern is
another.

PREPARING THE LAYERS

After transferring the design to the material, place the top
layer and the interlining together with wrong sides facing each
other. Match the raw edges and make sure the grain lines are in
perfect alignment. Baste the two layers together carefully so
they will be held securely in place.

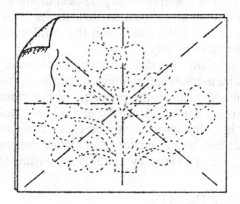

SEWING THE DESIGN

The stitches can be made by hand or machine. Usually hand
stitches create the most beautiful work and machine stitching
around delicate curves can be difficult.

Hand Sewing. Running stitches are usually used. Be sure to
keep them the same size and exactly the same distance apart.
If you are sewing on the underside of the finished piece, watch
carefully so that the effect is correct on the right side. You can
become so accustomed to just watching the effect on the right
side that you can forget that you are now working on the wrong
side.

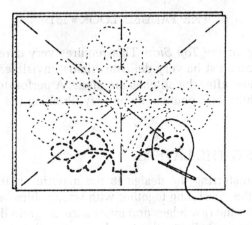

Backstitches can also be used, but unless you are working on the right side, you must be very careful of the appearance of the stitches. In fact it will probably be best if you work a stem stitch that will appear as a backstitch on the right side. The backstitch creates a bolder line than the running stitch, defining the design more clearly.

Machine Stitching. Set the machine for as small a straight stitch as can be made when sewing on the two layers of fabric you are using. Also check the pressure on the presser foot so the layers do not ride apart. At the end of the stitching, bring all the threads to the wrong side and tie ends securely.

Be sure that the stitches enclose completely the area that has to be padded. An open space will allow the batting to protrude.

PADDING THE DESIGN

After the design has been stitched by hand or machine, remove the basting stitches that run through it. Turn the work to the wrong side.

The Opening. If the interlining is loosely woven so the threads may be spread apart to make an opening, it will not be necessary to cut the material. Otherwise the fabric must be cut.

To do this, you must work carefully. You do not want to snip the top layer by mistake. Pinch a tiny fold in the interlining and at the center of the design. Make a small cut. If you find this difficult to do, slip a pin through the material at the point to be cut. The pin will help to guide the scissors and keep the layers apart.

Add the Padding. Place a small piece of batting through the opening. Push it into position, using the blunt end of a large needle, bodkin, or small scissors. Use enough padding to create the right effect, but not so much that the design is distorted, appearing hard and rigid. Instead, stuff it lightly but firmly with the batting, moving evenly into the corners and narrow areas so there is a certain puffy softness to the design.

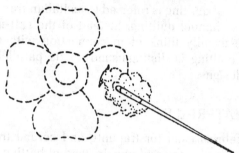

If the design has an area made up of two parallel lines, representing perhaps a stem, thread a blunt needle with a soft, heavy cotton rug yarn or bulky knitting yarn. Sometimes you may need to double the thread to fill the channel you are padding. Spread the fabric threads in the interfacing so the needle can be inserted between the rows of stitches.

When turning a definite curve, bring up the needle. Then insert the needle again at the same place, leaving the yarn slack. By doing this, the padding will not become taut, puckering the fabric.

Close the Opening. With the batting evenly distributed, sew the slit together with small whipstitches. Keep the stitches close together so the padding will not poke out between the stitches.

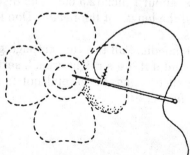

Continue to pad each part of the design in this way. When all sections have been completed, the design on the right side should stand out in a soft but bold relief.

Corded Quilting

This type of quilting is referred to as Italian trapunto and sometimes as channel quilting. Instead of the soft flowing designs that we usually think of in connection with trapunto work, corded quilting is distinguished by its parallel lines forming linear designs.

THE MATERIALS

The fabrics used for trapunto and corded trapunto are the same except for the padding. Instead of batting, a yarn or cord is employed. In case the filler you select might shrink when the article is laundered, be sure to preshrink it before using.

THE PROCEDURE

Follow the same procedure that you did for trapunto. Transfer the design to the fabric. Then baste the top and interlining together. Use tiny running stitches to sew the layers together along the design lines.

When the design has been defined with running stitches, thread a blunt needle or bodkin with yarn or cord. Insert the needle through a small opening in the channel formed by the two rows of stitches. Pass the needle through the channel for a short distance, about 1 inch (2.5 cm). The distance depends on the design and the length of the needle. Don't gather the fabric as you do this.

Bring up the needle. Pull the yarn through gently, allowing it to lie flat and taut if it is a straight area. Insert the needle again at the same exit opening. Be careful not to snag the yarn or penetrate the fabric.

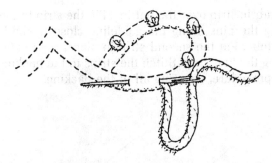

When turning a corner or following a curve, use the same procedure, but do not pull the filler taut. Instead, leave it slightly slack at the turning point. This allows for stretching when the article is in use, shrinkage when being laundered. It also prevents puckering, which occurs when the padding is too tight. Pulling the fabric gently on the bias, first one way and then another, will help to regulate the amount of yarn in each channel.

Strip Quilting with Stuffing

This type of quilting can also be given a three-dimensional look. Batting is cut in strips and enclosed as the strip is sewed in place.

Begin by making individual strips the width of the finished quilt. The depth of the strip will depend on the amount of stuffing you decide to use. Each strip can be made of a variety of colors and materials. Different textures are also suitable—cottons as well as velvet and satin can be used.

For the backing, select a fabric that seems appropriate for the material you are using for the strips. On the backing, draw lines that will indicate where to stitch the strips. The guidelines will keep the stitching straight.

Place the first strip on the backing with the right side down. Stitch pieces together.

Put a strip of batting on the backing along the stitching line.

Bring the fabric strip over the batting. Pin the strip to the backing, putting the pins along the guideline close to the batting, making a tube. Pin the second strip in place, right side down, overlapping the first strip. Stitch the strips to the backing. Continue this procedure, covering all of the backing.

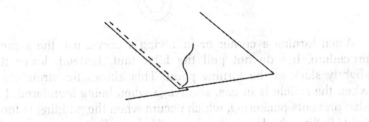

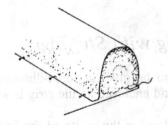

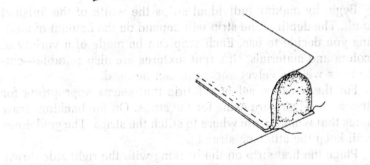

8

Quilting with Appliqué

It is hard to realize that the beautiful appliqué of today had its beginning as a utilitarian patch. Some historians tell us that when a whole-cloth quilt began to show wear in a certain spot a piece of fabric was added to cover it. Gradually the shape of the patches became more interesting. The geometric shapes evolved into realistic designs. Finally the French women introduced floral motifs, using velvets and satins in contrasting col-

ors. The plain quilt had taken on new elegance, creating a beautiful decorative touch in the home.

The earliest appliquéd quilts were made by assembling design motifs cut from printed chintzes and oriental calicoes on a white background, and then elaborately quilting it to bring out the details of the design in the printed fabric. Sometimes the quilts were given further ornamentation by the use of embroidery.

The appliquéd quilt became very popular in the United States during the nineteenth century. Appliquéing was used for making the "best" quilts in the household. The stitches were made meticulously, finely, and evenly; the designs were beautiful. So special was this type of quilt that appliquéd quilts were classified in various ways. Wedding, friendship, freedom, family-record, and album were some of the categories. Usually they were made as gifts for someone or something special.

The *album quilt* can be thought of as a picture book. Each block represented something of interest to the quilter. It might

have been a pictorial display of flowers, birds, or places or events in her town. Sometimes it was a simple representation of the alphabet. The *family-record quilt* displayed in the same fashion important events in the life of a family. Then there was the *freedom quilt*, made for a young man as a twenty-first birthday present. The *friendship quilt* was a highly prized gift. It was usually made by a group as a lasting remembrance for someone who was leaving a community, such as the minister.

For contemporary quilting, appliqué work can give the top a colorful and interesting look. Fanciful or realistic designs can have a feeling of the old, but with a new and distinctive air of today.

Design Suggestions

Just as an artist plans the design details of a painting, so must the quilter. The design can be simple and placed in a precise manner, or elaborate and scattered to produce a lovely pictorial motif. If you wish, you can just cut the designs from a patterned fabric; if you feel more creative, you can draw them yourself, producing an original motif. There are also patterns to buy and to trace.

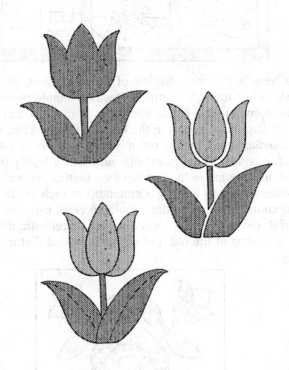

Sometimes the designs are made of only one piece, at others, they may be made of two or more parts, allowing for contrasts in color. It is also possible to group several designs to create a picturesque motif. Remember, you should think of yourself as a painter on fabric.

One type of original design may remind you of your childhood days when you cut out little paper doilies for your dolls. You can use that same method for cutting out symmetrical appliqué designs today. The patterns for traditional Hawaiian quilts are made this way.

You may find it helpful to browse through magazines for ideas. Greeting cards and coloring books offer other suggestions. Keep a file of hints. The designs can range from the whimsical to the very lovely.

If you are just beginning to do appliqué work, keep your designs simple. One-piece motifs with gentle curves will be best. Corners and sharp indentations and protrusions are difficult to handle.

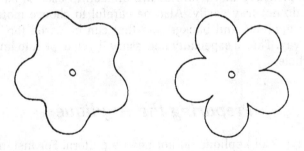

After you have planned a design, make a layout to show how it will look in its finished form. If the design is constructed in parts that have to be put together, be sure to number or letter each one. This makes it easier to fit them together on the background fabric. See top of next page.

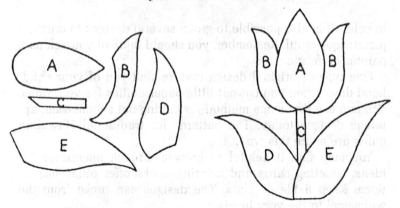

Fabrics. In planning the complete design, it is most important that you select fabrics in the right colors. A beautiful design can be ruined if the colors and fabrics are not appropriate.

Also select fabrics that are easy to handle. Smooth-surfaced materials in light to medium weight will be best. Loosely woven or heavy bulky fabrics are difficult to use. Be sure the edges do not fray easily. Also be careful to choose materials for the appliqué and background that can be cared for in the same way. This is especially necessary if you expect to launder the article.

Preparing the Appliqué

Some types of appliqué do not need a pattern. For instance, if you are using a patterned fabric for your motif, you have only to cut around it, leaving a margin of about 1 inch (2.5 cm). If you are not working with patterned material, you will need to make a pattern or template for the appliqué.

MAKING A PATTERN

Patterns can be prepared in various ways. The easiest way is to cut or trace a design that you like in a magazine, a book, a picture, or perhaps wallpaper. Then there are commercial patterns that you can purchase. If, however, you feel more cre-

ative and want something completely original, draw a design that seems appropriate or that you like.

Supplies. To transfer the design into a pattern, you will need paper, a pencil, scissors, and perhaps a ruler. The type of paper you use will depend on how it is to be used. If the pattern is to be traced around, over and over again, then you will need cardboard or illustration board. You do not want the pattern edges to become rough or worn. If the pattern is to be employed only a few times, brown wrapping paper of a sturdy quality is handy to have. If the design is to be traced from a book, you will need tracing paper. For changing the size of a design, graph paper in different sizes makes the conversion easier to do. Colored construction paper will be an aid in planning color schemes.

For cutting the paper, a pair of sharp scissors or shears is a "must." If it is impossible to cut accurately with scissors, try a razor-blade knife.

Of course you will need a pencil for tracing the pattern. If the design is made up of straight lines, you will find a ruler of great assistance.

Changing the Size. If you have chosen a design that is too small or too large for the project you are making, you can correct the size without too much trouble. It should be done before cutting out the pattern.

To enlarge the pattern, begin by tracing the design. Mark the tracing with a series of vertical and horizontal lines, forming squares or a grid. The lines must be drawn accurately with a ruler, a precise distance apart. The sizes of the squares can vary from 1/8 inch (3 mm) for a small design to 1 inch (2.5 cm) for a larger one. After you have the design divided in this way, decide how large the desired appliqué should be.

With this decision made, determine how many times the original design must be increased—twice the size or more. If you cannot find a graph paper with squares in the right size, you will have to make your own.

On a large sheet of paper, such as brown wrapping paper, draw vertical and horizontal lines the correct distance apart. For instance, if you want the design to be double the original size, then the squares should be drawn twice as large. A 1/4-inch (6-mm) square will become a 1/2-inch (1.3-cm) square. Copy the design outline on the graph paper, transferring it from the smaller squares to the corresponding larger ones.

To *decrease the pattern,* follow the same procedure, but instead of making the squares larger on the graph paper, draw them smaller.

QUILTING WITH APPLIQUÉ • 145

Cutting the Pattern. Do this carefully. Cut precisely on the penciled lines, using sharp scissors that you use only for cutting paper. Number or label all the pieces so they correspond to their counterparts in your original design plan.

Folding a Pattern. Another way to create a pattern is by folding a sheet of paper before cutting out the design, just as you did when you were little. It creates a symmetrical design that is easily made.

Work with a square made of lightweight but durable paper. The size depends on what you are making. For a quilt block, you might try a square 12 to 18 inches (30.5 to 46 cm).

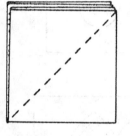

Fold the paper square in half, matching the edges, then in half again, and once more if you wish. The folded paper is now in a triangular shape. Be sure to crease the folds sharply so each section is the same size. If you have trouble folding the paper, run your ruler along the edge.

Draw the design on one section between the folds. Cut along the design lines. When you open the square, you have four identical units radiating from the center.

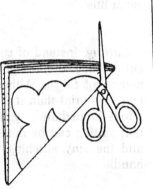

TRANSFERRING THE DESIGN

Before tracing the design on the material, press the fabric. Place the material on a firm surface with the right side up and smooth it out.

If you are working with a printed fabric, position the design carefully so the effect will be attractive when the appliqué is applied to the background material. There may be a dominant design detail or spot of color that will influence the resulting look. Check the grain lines. The grain lines in the appliqué should follow the grain lines in the background piece.

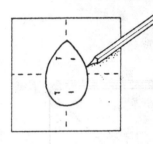

Pin the paper pattern in place. Do not put it too close to the edge or selvage. Trace around the edge with a well-sharpened pencil. Draw with a sharp and accurate line. It is important that the shape remain exact so the resulting appliqué will be perfect. The line becomes the seam line. If you are using a cardboard pattern, just hold the piece in place and mark around it.

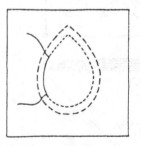

MAKING THE APPLIQUÉ

After tracing the design on the fabric, remove the pattern. Indicate the placement of the cutting line by marking the seam allowance 1/4 inch (6 mm) from the seam line.

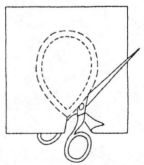

Cutting. Instead of cutting on this line, cut outside the design lines, leaving a margin of fabric. Although you will use more material than if you cut out the appliqué immediately, you will find the actual cutting can be done more accurately and the stay stitching will be easier to handle.

Stay Stitching. Although the application of the appliqué can be done without stay stitching, this does have certain advantages. It controls the shape more accurately and allows the seam allowance to be clipped closer to the seam line. With the machine set for 12 to 15 stitches per inch (2.5 cm), stitch in the seam allowance, just outside the marked seam line.

Clipping. Cut out the appliqué on the outside marked line. Clip the curved seam allowances with well-sharpened scissors, using only the points. Make the clip perpendicular to the seam line—just to it, never through it. Place the clips close together when the curves are sharp, and farther apart when the curves are very gentle, almost straight. In case the design has a narrow space between two parts, snip straight down into the indentation. Treat an inside corner in the same way. For an outside corner, cut off the point.

The Background. To make it easier to apply the appliqué in the correct position, fold the fabric piece in half. Press lightly. Then fold it in half horizontally and diagonally, pressing lightly after each folding. Use these pressed lines as guides.

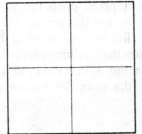
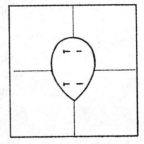

Attaching the Appliqué

Applying the appliqué to the background fabric can be done by hand, by machine, or by fusing. Here it is a matter of preference. Do you want something sturdy and practical that you can do quickly, or instead something fine and beautiful? Each can be attractive, but in a different way.

BY HAND

Again there is a decision to make—how to handle the seam allowance. There are two methods to use. The seam allowance can be turned under and basted in place before the sewing begins, or the turning under can be done as the stitches are made. The first method takes a little more time in the preparation, but it makes the actual sewing easier to do and assures a more perfect contour to the finished design.

Basting. Just as in sewing, baste with a regular sewing needle and thread in a contrasting color. Working on the wrong side, turn the seam allowance toward you. As you baste, fold the material carefully on the penciled or stay-stitched line. Use small stitches. Check frequently to see that the outline on the right side follows the design contour perfectly and the clipped sections are tucked under securely. If you stay-stitched the appliqué, be sure that the stitched line does not show on the right side.

Sewing. Before pinning the basted appliqué in place, press the background material but not the appliqué. Place the material flat on a smooth, firm surface. Position the appliqué carefully. Use diagonal basting stitches to hold it in place. Remove the pins. To ensure the accurate placement of the appliqué on the background fabric, trace the motif on it.

The stitches used to hold the appliqué in place should be invisible, allowing the folded edge to produce a rolled effect. A slip stitch works nicely. Move the needle through the fold, picking up two or three threads in the background material. Several stitches can be loaded onto the needle before pulling the needle and thread through the fabric. At points where the fabric may fray, take tiny overhand stitches to reinforce these areas. Be careful that the needle does not penetrate the top surface. Working with matching thread will also help to conceal the stitches.

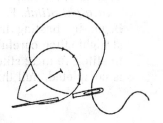

Without basting under the seam allowance, pin the appliqué into place and baste. Be careful that the basting stitches are not placed too close to the seam line or extend into the seam allowance. Remember that the seam allowance has to be turned under.

Using the point of your needle, roll the seam allowance under as you make a slip stitch. If there is stay stitching around the motif, be sure it is not visible on the right side. Continue to sew in this way until appliqué is securely in place. Remove the basting stitches.

BY MACHINE

Except for using machine stitches in place of slip stitches, the procedures for machine appliqués duplicate those employed for hand appliqué. The seam allowances can be turned under or left flat. If you decide to fold under the edges, take special care to keep the seam allowances even, with a smooth outer edge. Straight or zigzag stitching can be used for sewing the appliqué in place.

Straight Stitch. For a folded edge, sew with a straight stitch. Begin by basting the appliqué in place. Then sew with a straight stitch carefully along the folded edge. Set the machine to stitch 10 to 12 stitches per inch (2.5 cm). When the stitching is completed, pull the thread ends to the underside and tie.

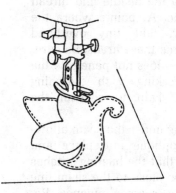

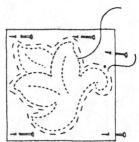

Zigzag Stitches. After the appliqué has been basted in place, put a row of straight machine stitches around the motif. There are two ways to handle the stitching. The line of straight machine stitches can be covered with small zigzag stitches and the material trimmed away close to the stitching, or the seam allowance can be cut away close to the stitching line before the zigzag stitches are made.

For both methods, cover the stitching line and raw edges with closely placed zigzag stitches. Before starting to stitch, test the stitches for the correct length and width to obtain the correct effect. Stitch slowly for the best results.

At the end of the stitching line, do not overlap the stitches. Pull the threads to the underside and tie the ends. Remove the basting stitches.

BY FUSING

Certain types of quilted articles do not require appliqués that are attached with tiny stitches. A fusible web can be used instead. Although it is easy and quick to use, it does produce a certain amount of stiffness, which isn't always attractive. So that you will be sure of the results, test it. Follow the manufacturer's directions exactly. Unless you do, the bonding of the two fabrics may not be perfect. The two layers will come apart when the article is laundered.

Begin by pinning the wrong side of the appliqué material to the fusing web. You should think of the two layers as one. Pin

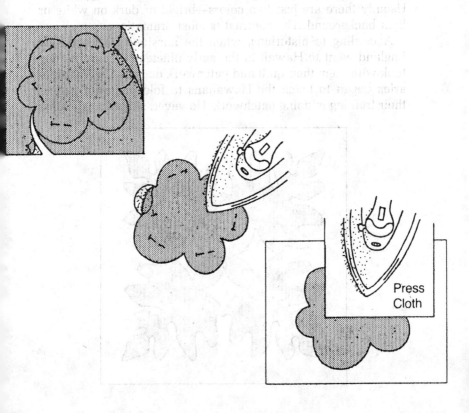

Press Cloth

the pattern to the right side of the fabric. Trace the outline carefully. Cut out the two layers on the marked line.

Smooth out the background material with the right side up. Position the appliqué so the grain lines are in perfect alignment and pin. Then, carefully following the directions that accompany the webbing, press with a heated iron. Start at the center area and work toward the edges. Remove the pins as you press. Do not press over them or slide the iron as you press. Instead lift the iron and move it to another area. Be sure the edges are firmly bonded.

Hawaiian-Style Appliqué

Designs created in Hawaii have a very special look. The colors are striking and the designs lavish with naturalistic patterns. Usually there are just two colors—bright or dark on white or light background. The contrast is most dramatic.

According to historians, when the missionaries from New England went to Hawaii in the early nineteenth century, they took with them their quilt and patchwork designs. The missionaries began to teach the Hawaiians to fold paper as part of their training in doing patchwork. However, since the islanders

did not wear clothes, they did not have small bits of leftover fabric to use. All they had were large pieces of tapa cloth that they used for bedding. One day a creative person folded a piece of paper as she had been taught and cut out a design that she had seen—a shadow of a palm tree. It was the beginning of a very beautiful type of appliqué work.

THE PATTERN

Before undertaking a design for a large project, work with a small one. Start with an 8-inch (20.5-cm) square of paper. Fold it in half, then in quarters so you have a 4-inch (10-cm) square, and finally in half again so that a triangular-shaped piece remains. If you unfold the paper, you will notice that you have eight triangular sections radiating from a center point. They should duplicate each other exactly in size.

Return the square to its folded form. With the point toward you, draw a simple design on the paper. Remember, simple designs are easier to appliqué than are delicate, lacy ones, and they can be most effective.

Draw half of the design on one edge and the other half on the other one with some detail between. Cut out the design, holding the folds tightly and firmly together. To be sure the design is exactly the way you want it, open it up. If you want to make it more decorative, refold and cut some more. Be careful not to cut along the folded edge. When you have the design exactly as you want it, you can convert it into the size you need for your project. Suggestions for increasing the size of a design pattern are given on page 144.

If you are making a large article such as a quilt, you will have to increase the size of the pattern considerably. To do this, decide on the final size. If you are making a quilt to use on a double bed, then a 90-inch (229-cm) square will cover it nicely. Instead of making a pattern 90 inches (229 cm) square, work with a 45-inch (114.5-cm) piece of paper, just a quarter of the needed size. Heavy wrapping paper works well.

Fold the square in half diagonally. Draw the design on the paper and cut.

To transfer the design to the fabric requires precision. Unless the large piece of material is folded exactly, the design will not be perfectly balanced. Begin by cutting a 90-inch (229-cm) square of fabric. In order to avoid seamed material, use sheets for both the design and the backing.

Fold the square of cloth as you did the small paper pattern. Pin the folds together securely. Place the pattern on the material and pin carefully. Leaving a 1/4-inch (6-mm) seam line, cut out the pattern through all layers of fabric. You will need sharp shears to do this accurately. Remove the pattern and pins. Open up the appliqué, which should be in one piece, ready to be placed on the background.

To center the appliqué accurately, fold the background in half vertically, horizontally, and diagonally. Press the fold line lightly. If the creases seem indefinite, baste them. The lines will act as guidelines.

Place the background square on the floor or on a large table with the right side up. Smooth it out, holding it taut with masking tape. Unfold the appliqué gently. Put it on the background with the right side up. Match the guidelines carefully, starting with the center line. Be careful not to stretch the fabric out of shape as you work. Pin and baste the appliqué in place with great care.

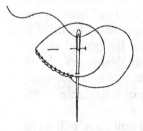

The edges of the appliqué can be handled in the usual manner by turning under the seam allowance and securing the fold with slip stitches. However, if you find it difficult to maneuver around a lacy design, you may use tiny embroidery stitches. The appliqué remains flat after the seam allowance is removed. Stitches

cover the raw edge. Blanket and herringbone stitches produce a good effect. If
matching thread and very small stitches
are used, the sewing is almost invisible.

Border Design. Sometimes a decorative border is needed.
The design can be cut from folded paper as was the center
motif. In fact it is possible to cut the center and border patterns
from the same folded square. Follow the same preparation

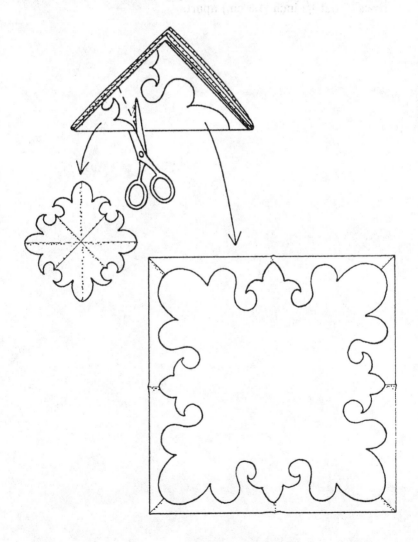

techniques as you did for making the center motif. Experiment with a small design before attempting a large one.

After folding the square, draw a line about one third the distance from the point. Use the upper portion for drawing the border design and the lower portion for the center motif. Cutting on the two design lines will produce three sections.

Usually the appliqué is surrounded with rows of contour quilting. The stitches follow the outline of the appliqué with the rows about 1/2 inch (1.3 cm) apart.

9

Patchwork Piecing

When I was a little girl I heard my grandmothers mention "piecing a quilt." I never heard the word "patchwork" used. Later I realized that when a pieced design created a geometric pattern it was referred to as patchwork.

Piecing was fun for a little girl to watch. There always seemed to be a story for each swatch Grandmother pulled from the ragbag, as Grandmother called it. Mother had a dress of this, a favorite aunt a blouse of that, and sometimes there would be a piece from something I had worn. The "silk quilt" was my favorite. The colors were so beautiful, the feel so soft.

Pieced work produces different looks and utilizes a variety of techniques. Patchwork is one of them. Shaped pieces of fabric are sewn together to produce a larger unit. The joined pieces can create a variety of designs that promote neatness and vitality. Some designs are simple and easy to diagram, others so complex that it is difficult to find the parts.

Origin of Patchwork

Patchwork seems to have evolved in America through necessity. Thrifty and ingenious settlers who had little soon found themselves adding bits of material to a quilt to cover worn spots. Fabrics were used and reused. Gradually the plain quilts took on a completely new look. Instead of just adding patches to prolong the life of a quilt, small pieces of cloth were sewn together to form a larger, decorative piece of fabric. This was the beginning of patchwork in New England. As the settlers moved westward they began to call this type of needlework "pieced work."

The art of patchwork flourished for about a hundred years, from 1775 to 1875. At first the small pieces were sewn directly onto a cloth backing. Sewing hundreds and sometimes thousands of tiny pieces together this way was tedious and handling them difficult. This led to a more efficient method in about 1800. The pieces were sewn together to form a block or square that was part of a total design plan. The blocks were then sewn together in rows or diagonal bands. Strips of fabric, forming a lattice effect, or plain blocks, alternating between the patterned ones and creating a frame for the patchwork, added interest to the quilt.

Soon new designs appeared. Some were original; others were adaptations of familiar ones. Inspiration for the design and its name often came from political and social events. Sometimes a pattern was given several names and, at others, the same name was given to several unrelated designs. The variations seem to be the result of quilters living in widely separated regions.

Today, when you review a pattern and its name, it is often difficult to see the correlation between the two. The names are often so quaint and whimsical that you wish you knew something about the person who thought of the name and created the design.

General Directions

In assembling the various shapes, a block, usually a square, is produced. It can be used singly or combined with other blocks, forming an all-over pattern for a larger piece.

THE BLOCK

Generally the blocks are pieced so the geometric design produces a balanced effect. The arrangement of the pieces, how-

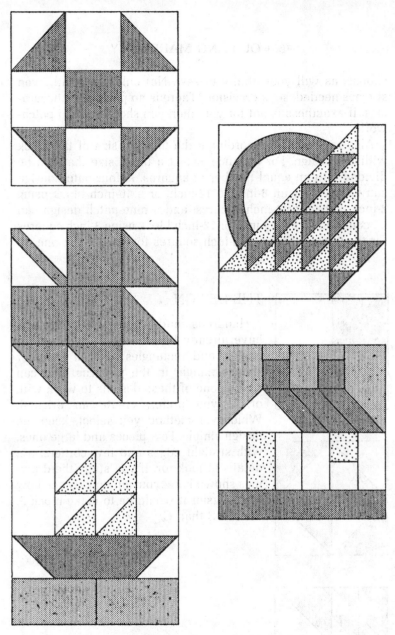

ever, can produce visual effects such as leaves, flowers, houses.

Before beginning to piece a block, you should decide how it is to be used. This will influence the design and the size you choose, as will your ability to sew. Not only are small, even stitches needed, so is precision. There is no place for inaccuracies. If exactness is not for you, then you should not do patchwork.

Also remember to coordinate the finished size of the block with the design. For instance, select a block size that can be divided into an equal number of squares. A four-patch design can be used for an 8-inch, a 12-inch, or a 16-inch block using 2-inch, 3-inch, or 4-inch squares, and a nine-patch design can be constructed as a 9-inch or 12-inch block using 3-inch squares for the 9-inch block and 4-inch squares for the 12-inch one.

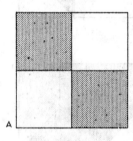

A

THE DESIGN

Hundreds and hundreds of designs have already been created. Squares, triangles, and rectangles as well as other shapes mingle in the patterns. You can choose one of these designs to work with or, if you prefer, create an original. Whichever method you select, keep the design simple. Few pieces and large ones, with straight edges and few corners, are details to look for. If you study the drawings shown here, you can quickly see how much easier it would be to make block A than B, B than C.

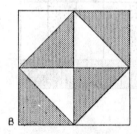

B

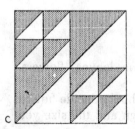

C

Folding a Pattern. Have you ever wondered how the early quilters did their designing? They didn't have supplies such as paper, pencils, and rulers, which we take for granted. Instead they folded scraps of paper into squares, triangles, and other geometric shapes. Why don't you try the technique the early quilters used to design their blocks? It will help you understand how a pattern evolved.

Folding a Four-Patch. Work with a piece of paper 12 inches (30.5 cm) square. Fold it in half lengthwise and then crosswise so you have four smaller squares (A). This design is referred to as a Four-Patch.

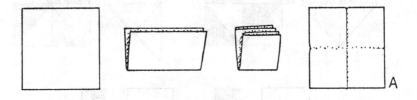

Then if you fold two opposite corners toward the center, the design takes on a new look. Two triangles have been added (B). If you make the block in contrasting colors, notice how different it appears.

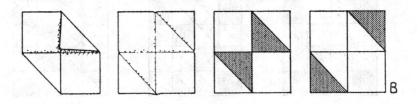

For another look, fold the other corners (C). By folding the original square from corner to corner, still another look appears. By ignoring squares and concentrating on triangles, other designs are produced. By continuing to subdivide the larger and smaller squares and by arranging the contrasts in materials and colors, you can achieve patterns like those shown here.

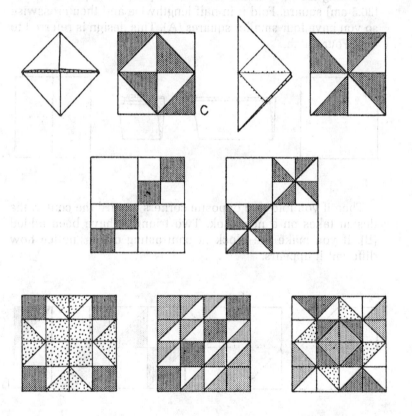

Folding a Nine-Patch. It is sometimes referred to as a three-patch and is probably the best-known patchwork pattern. Instead of folding the square in half, you fold it in thirds. When you open the paper up, you find that you have nine small squares.

If you just add color you can create designs such as those shown here. However, if you decide to transform some of the squares into triangles, then looks such as these can be produced.

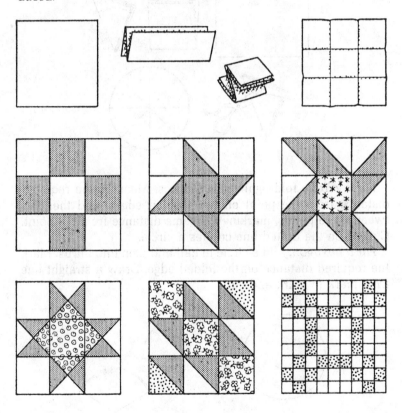

Folding Other Geometrics. Circles, hexagons, and stars can also be produced through folding. For each of these forms, fold a square into halves. Crease the folds firmly and accurately. Pinch the point.

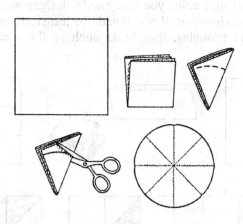

For a circle, fold again into squares. Measure the required distance from the point on both folded edges, and then between these points, marking the same distance from the point. Cutting on the dotted line creates a circle.

For a hexagon, fold a circle in half and then into thirds. Mark the required distance on the folded edge. Draw a straight line from mark to mark and cut.

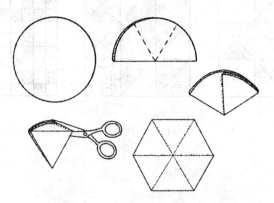

For a simple star, fold the square into quarters. Then place the folded edges together, right to left, forming a triangle. Fold the triangle in half again, and then the tip down as indicated by the dotted line on the diagram. When you open up the pattern, you will have the design shown here.

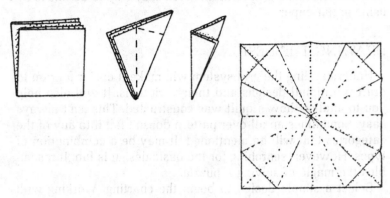

For a four-pointed star, fold the square as you did for a simple star. But instead of holding the folded point for the final creasing, hold the opposite or open point. After folding as indicated by the accompanying drawing, turn down the point. When you open the square, you will find a star with a square in the center.

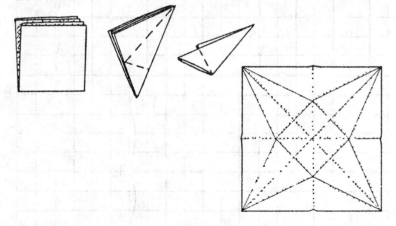

Grid. As you unfolded each square, did you notice that the creases produced a pattern of vertical and horizontal lines that formed a series of squares of uniform size? This frame is referred to as a grid. All of the designs you have just folded can be transferred to a grid formation. An easy way to do this is by using graph paper.

DRAWING THE DESIGN

Understanding the grid system will make it easier for you to draft traditional designs and their variations. It will also help you to analyze how a quilt was constructed. This isn't always easy. Sometimes an all-over pattern doesn't fall into any of the categories that will be mentioned. It may be a combination of types. However, searching for the basic design is fun. It resembles the magic of solving a puzzle.

Select a simple design to begin the charting. Working with graph paper with larger squares will make the task easier.

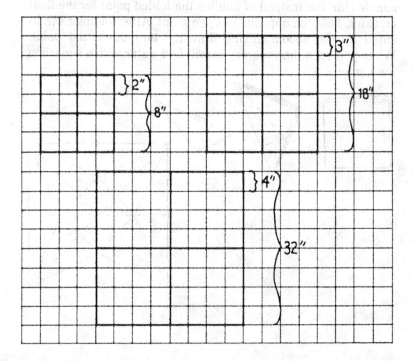

Four-patch grid designs are the simplest to make. From your folding experience, you know it is based on four squares of equal size. Because it is so simple in design, each square is usually divided into four smaller ones, producing sixteen squares. Sometimes the repeat units are the same, allowing for variations in placement; at others, the repeat units can be different.

Nine-patch grid designs, sometimes referred to as three-patch, are perhaps the most commonly seen. The pattern is made up of three squares across and three squares down. These squares can be subdivided to produce the desired pattern.

Five-patch grid designs are made up of twenty-five squares —five squares across the top and five squares down the side. This formation allows for more complicated designs. Sometimes the arrangement creates a band through the center that eventually produces a lattice effect.

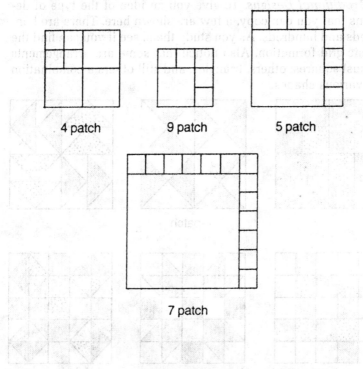

4 patch   9 patch   5 patch

7 patch

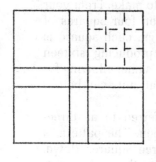

Seven-patch grid designs are based on a composition of seven squares across the top and seven squares down, or a total of forty-nine squares. This allows a nine-patch square to be tucked into each corner, and the spaces between to be converted into bands. If you study the drawing shown here, you can understand this arrangement more clearly. An intersecting parallel-line block pattern has been created.

Sometimes diagonal lines are used to divide a square from corner to corner. These lines often act as a basis for a design. Instead of squares there are triangles to be subdivided, creating the patterns.

Traditional Designs. To give you an idea of the type of designs that you can copy, a few are shown here. There are hundreds and hundreds. As you study them, see if you can find the basic grid formation. Also notice that some are arrangements of just squares; others, triangles, and still others a combination of various shapes.

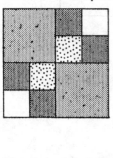
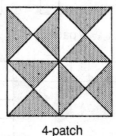
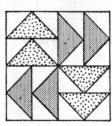

4-patch

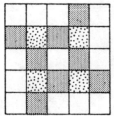
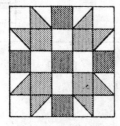
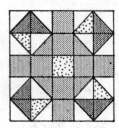

5-patch

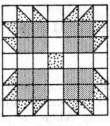

7-patch

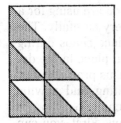 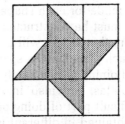 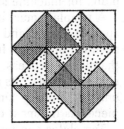

9-patch

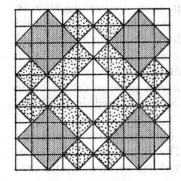 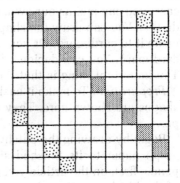

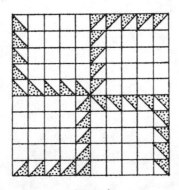

10-patch

TEMPLATES

The pattern pieces needed for patchwork are called templates. The size depends on whether they are being used for hand or machine stitching. When the pieces are to be sewn together by hand, the template is known as a marking template; for machine stitching, a cutting template.

A template must be made for each shape you are using for a specific design, and it must be constructed very carefully. The slightest deviation from the perfect will produce chaos during the piecing process. Each piece has its special place in the design and must fit its adjoining piece exactly. This precision, not only in making templates, but also in cutting and sewing pieces, is the most difficult part of doing patchwork.

Templates can be obtained in different ways. First, you can buy them. This isn't always easy to do if you don't live in an area where there is a store that sells quilting supplies. In such a case, you can make your own. Again, there are various ways to do this. You can draw the shape on graph paper, cut it out, and paste it to cardboard. Or you can draw the shape directly onto cardboard. You can decide which method works best for you. The important thing is that the final results be good.

Preparation. To make it easier for you, patterns for the basic shapes are shown here. They can be reproduced on graph paper.

Begin by drawing the patchwork block you want to make on graph paper to its finished size. The size of each shape depends, first, on the article you are making, and then on the size of the block you are using.

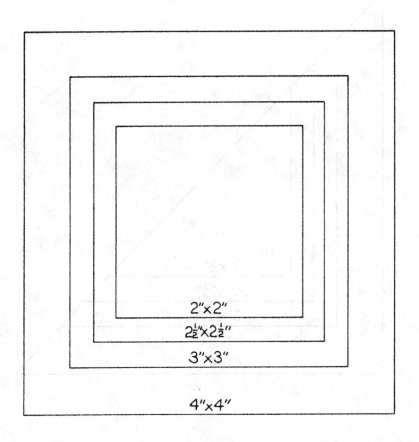

2"×2"

2½"×2½"

3"×3"

4"×4"

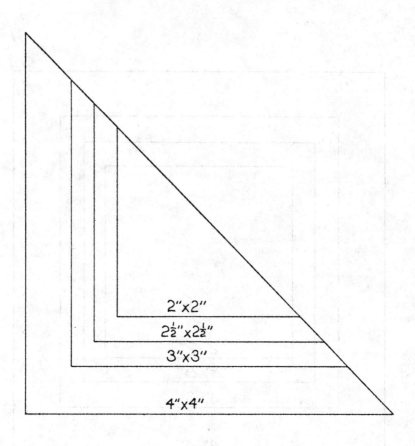

2"x2"

2½"x2½"

3"x3"

4"x4"

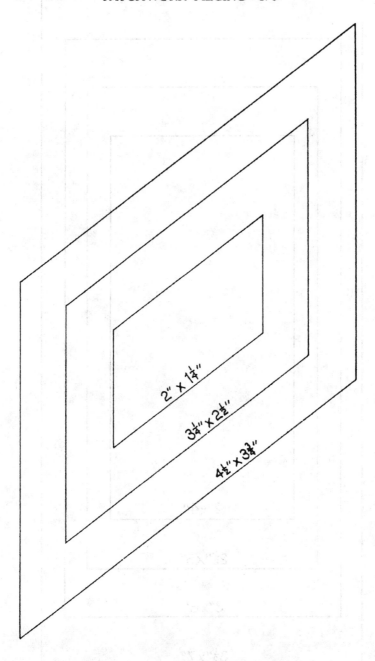

$2'' \times 1\frac{1}{4}''$

$3\frac{1}{4}'' \times 2\frac{1}{2}''$

$4\frac{1}{2}'' \times 3\frac{3}{4}''$

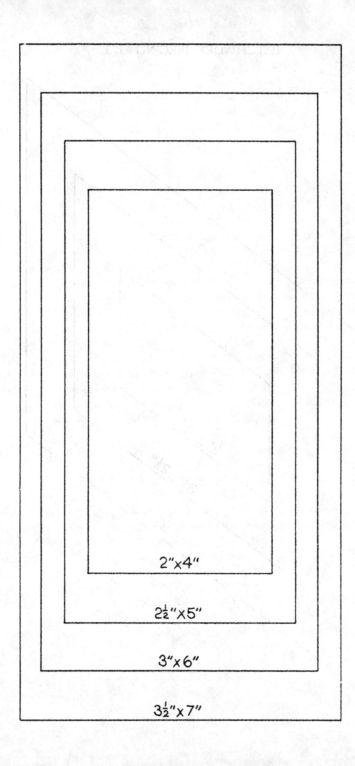

2"x4"

2½"x5"

3"x6"

3½"x7"

Decide how many different templates you will need. Cut out one of each shape. For instance, for the basic nine-patch block you will need just a square, but for the Shoofly pattern a triangle as well as a square will be required.

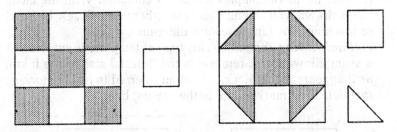

Transferring the Shape. After cutting out the shape, you are ready to transfer it to heavier paper. This can be done by pasting the paper shape to the heavier material or by tracing around the design.

There are many materials from which to choose. Some quilters prefer a single-thickness cardboard or illustration board; others, a fine sandpaper. Actually the material depends on how many times the template is to be used. Lighter materials, such as poster board, are all right for a small project, but heavier material, such as double-thickness illustration board, will be

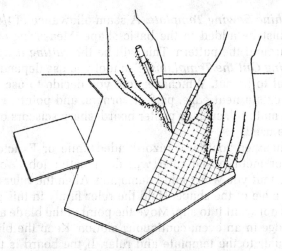

better when it is necessary to trace around it hundreds of times. You don't want the edges to become ragged.

Some quilters prefer to draft the shapes directly on the board, using pencil and ruler. At times, they use a plastic triangle and, for more complex shapes, a compass. With the basic shape drawn, you should decide whether you will sew by hand or machine. The templates are different.

Hand Sewing Template. This type of template is cut without a seam allowance. It represents the finished size of the fabric as it appears in the block. It is often referred to as the *marking template*. The marked line is the sewing line.

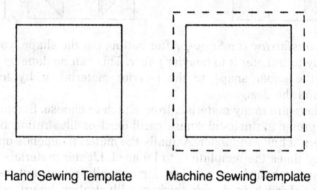

Hand Sewing Template   Machine Sewing Template

Machine Sewing Template. A seam allowance of 1/4 inch (6 mm) must be added to the basic shape. Measuring carefully, draw around the pattern. This will be the *cutting template*.

Cutting Out the Templates. The tool you use depends on the material to be cut. Whichever tool you decide to use, be sure that it cuts a neat edge, perfect corners, and points. For lightweight material, such as poster board, sharp scissors or shears may be used.

For heavier boards, a razor-bladed knife or Exacto plus a metal or metal-edged ruler will do a better job. Work on a surface that you won't mind damaging. Align the ruler with the drawn edge of the shape. Hold the ruler firmly in this position. You do not want it to slip. Move the point of the blade along the ruler edge in an even, continuous motion. Keep the blade perpendicular to the template and ruler. If the board is thick, do

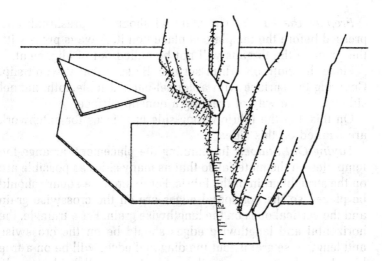

not attempt to cut through it the first time. Repeat the motion until you make a smooth cut.

Some templates that can be used for both marking and cutting are available. They look like small frames with hollow centers. The marking line is on the inside; the cutting line on the outside, with the seam allowance between.

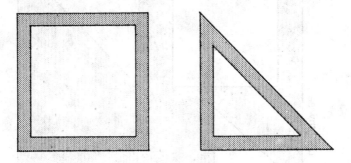

MARKING THE FABRIC

Again accuracy is most important. Although the template may be perfectly cut, a slip of the pencil will spoil the results.

Prepare the Fabric. The material should be preshrunk and pressed before the template is placed on it. Always press with the grain so the threads will not be pulled out of alignment.

Place the cloth on a firm surface. Be sure that it won't slip. Covering the surface with a flannel-backed tablecloth, flannel side up, is one way of creating a nonslip surface.

On this, lay the fabric wrong side up. Pieces for patchwork are marked on this side.

Laying Out Shapes. In planning the placement, arrange the templates on the material so that as many sides as possible are on the straight grain of the fabric. For example, a square should be placed so the horizontal edges are on the crosswise grain and the vertical ones on the lengthwise grain. For a triangle, the horizontal and lengthwise edges should be on the crosswise and lengthwise grains, but the diagonal edges will be on a true bias. For a diamond or parallelogram, two parallel sides should be put on the lengthwise grain. Bias edges make it more difficult to ensure a perfect fit.

Crosswise

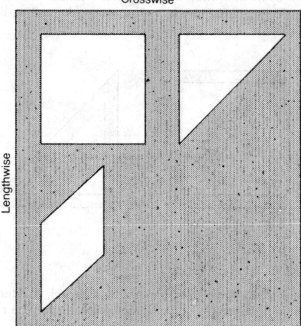

Lengthwise

For *hand sewing*, a space of 1/2 inch (1.3 cm) is left between the shapes. This provides a 1/4-inch (6-mm) seam allowance for the template you are about to mark and the ones adjoining it. You will use the marking template you made. The line you mark is the sewing line.

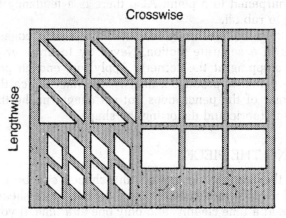

For *machine sewing*, place the shapes so no space is left between them. Use the cutting template. The line you mark is the cutting line.

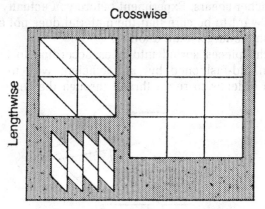

The Marking. Use a well-sharpened number 2 pencil. You may have to sharpen the pencil frequently. Unless the point is sharp, you will not make a sharp, well-defined line. A blunt pencil may enlarge the size of each piece as much as 1/8 inch (3 mm).

If you are working on a fabric on which the pencil markings do not show, try a dressmaker's white chalk or artist's white drawing pencil. It will be difficult to keep the dressmaker's pencil sharpened to a point. Also there is a tendency for the marking to rub off.

Hold the template firmly in place. Mark each edge of the template in a separate motion. Never try to draw around it without stopping at the corners. Apply just enough pressure with the pencil to produce a fine, visible line. Watch that the sharp point of the pencil does not get caught in the threads, pulling the fabric and distorting the shape.

CUTTING THE PIECE

With the marking completed, the shapes can be cut out. Again do this precisely with sharp dressmaker's shears. Cut one edge at a time cleanly, and only one at a time. If you have marked for hand sewing, remember to leave the margin around the shapes.

Some quilters are able to cut several layers of fabric at once, using Gingher shears. Experiment before you actually try to do this. You want to be sure that the material does not slip, making one shape larger than another.

Keep the pieces sorted into piles according to shape and color. An old-fashioned but still efficient way to keep the pieces in order is to run a thread through the center of each stack.

SEWING THE PIECES

Before the piecing begins, plan the sequence for sewing. Never join the pieces in a haphazard fashion. Small units of the design are first to be made, and then they are joined to construct a larger one.

Plan the Sequence. For the nine-patch pattern, Shoofly, four smaller units of two triangles each are first sewn together, making a square. These squares are then combined with other squares to form three rows. The rows are then joined with two parallel seams.

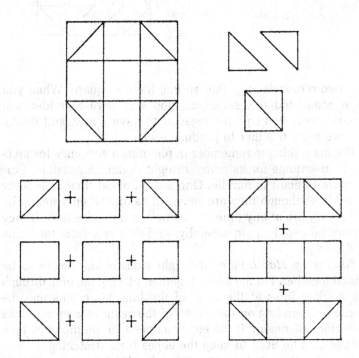

For the Four-Patch, Dutchman's Puzzle, two large triangles and four small ones are needed for each unit. Begin by sewing two small triangles to each larger one to form a rectangle. Then

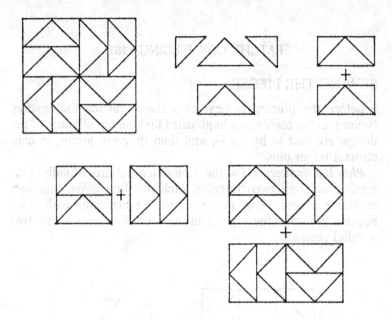

join two rectangles together so you have a square. When you have completed this sequence, you will have four identical squares. Sew two squares together to have a row, and finally the two rows together to produce a block.

The main thing to remember in planning a sequence for piecing is to arrange for as many straight seams as possible. Corners are difficult to handle. One should avoid them whenever possible. Although they are easier to handle when seaming by hand, they are at any time an obstacle to a precise look. If they cannot be avoided, pin carefully, and then sew from the angle to the edge.

Sewing by Hand. Place the right sides of the pieces to be joined together. Pin the edges together, placing the pins through the marked lines at the ends of the line. More pins may be needed, depending on the length of the seam to keep the lines in perfect alignment. If the edge has been cut on the bias, then pins should be used to keep the edges from stretching.

A sewing thread about 12 to 18 inches (30.5 cm to 46 cm) long works well. Longer lengths have a tendency to knot and tangle. At the end of the thread, a knot can be placed.

To make the plain seam, start by inserting the threaded sewing needle through both pieces of fabric at the beginning of both penciled marking lines. Sew with a tiny, even running stitch. Check frequently to be sure that the needle is penetrating the seam line on the underside exactly. Remove the pins as you work. End the row of stitches at the end of the marked line with several backstitches.

Pressing. Although seams are pressed after being made in sewing, it isn't always done in patchwork. Some quilters prefer to wait until the block is completed. Instead of the seam being pressed open, it is pressed to one side. By waiting, you can press in the direction that produces the best effect, so seams will not show and points will not be too bulky. Remember, dark fabrics should not be pressed under light ones. The effect would not be pleasing. Work first on the wrong side and then on the right side, using a press cloth.

Joining Rows. After placing the right sides of two rows together, anchor the ends of the marked line with a pin. Insert the pin perpendicular to the line. Slip another pin through the seam line at the point where the piecing seams meet. It is most important that points or corners meet exactly. Slip the pin through each of the pieces in both rows by catching one or two threads.

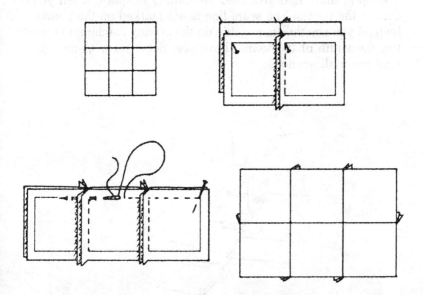

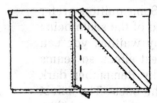

Make a plain seam with running stitches along the seam line. Remove the pins as you sew. Whether to sew the seam allowance down depends on the number of seams to be crossed. If only three or four pieces are involved at a point, and the thickness of the layers does not interfere with the size and evenness of the stitches, the seam allowance can be pressed to one side and sewn in place. However if six or more layers meet, it is better not to try to sew them down. It is just too difficult to push the needle through so many pieces of material.

Machine Piecing. Contemporary quilts are often made by piecing the blocks by machine and then holding the three layers of material together with handmade quilting stitches. This combination of techniques makes patchwork quicker to do and results in a stronger product.

Keep in mind that you used the cutting template when you cut out the pieces. The seam line is not marked on the pieces. Instead you use the seam guide on the sewing machine to control the width of the seam allowance. Set it for a 1/4-inch (6-mm) seam allowance.

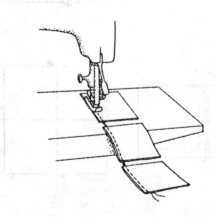

Work with cotton-covered polyester thread, setting the machine for 12 stitches per inch (2.5 cm).

Pin the pieces together as you did for sewing by hand. Stitch the seam, beginning at the edge of the piece to the opposite one. To make the stitching less time-consuming, don't end the stitching at this point. Continue to stitch the next unit. Stitch carefully so the seams will be straight and even.

Before the units can be joined, the seams should be pressed. Pin the pressed pieces together, giving special attention to the crossing seams. Match the seam lines, edges, points, or corners carefully so each detail meets accurately. When the block is completed, give it a final pressing.

English Paper Patchwork

Working with paper offers another way to do patchwork. It is a method that was widely used in Great Britain for centuries and for that reason is sometimes spoken of as English quilting. The paper becomes the tool for achieving perfection in the construction, not a part of the finished product.

Paper templates are covered with fabric and then sewn together with a whipstitch. After the pieces are in place, the paper is removed. It is a technique that works nicely when joining such shapes as diamonds and hexagons, as well as when you are constructing a block with various-shaped pieces with many corners as in the house design shown here.

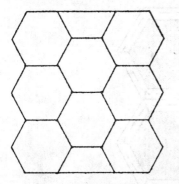
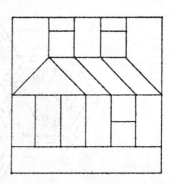

Paper. Begin by making the template in the required shape. You will need a marking template without the seam allowances. Using paper the weight of notebook paper, draw carefully around the template. The weight of the paper is controlled by the weight of the fabric. If you are using a fabric heavier than the usual quilting material, you may need a firmer paper, perhaps an index card.

Preparing the Patch. Cut out the paper piece carefully. Use sharp scissors, making sure that you cut accurately. It will be impossible to fit the pieces together exactly unless you do.

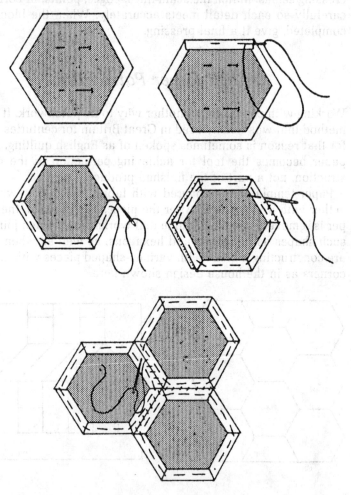

Pin the paper piece to the wrong side of the fabric. Plan for the pieces as you do for regular pieced work, being mindful of the grain lines. Be sure to leave a seam allowance of 1/4 inch (6 mm) around each piece. As you cut, be certain that the paper does not slip.

Fold the fabric over the paper. Keep the 1/4-inch (6-mm) seam allowance even. Baste in place. It is best to start at the widest angle. Sharp points may require extra folding.

Sew the pieces together with tiny whipstitches placed very close to the folded edge. This allows the work to be opened up so it lies flat. With right sides together, match the edges precisely.

Work with a regular sewing needle and thread. Matching the thread to the darker fabric usually works nicely.

After the pieces have been sewn together, remove the basting stitches and paper. In case the stitches have passed through the paper, gently pull the paper away.

Finish by pressing. In this type of patchwork, the seams are pressed open.

Medallion Quilting

Sometimes tops are pieced with a central motif dominating the design plan. The effect has the look of a large block framed with several borders. Although the central medallion is usually made of a single piece of fabric, there are times when several small blocks are grouped together to create this outstanding look.

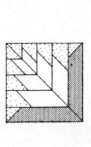
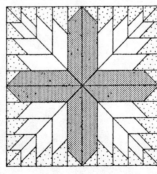

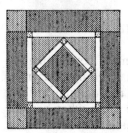

In constructing this type of top, you work in a different fashion. You begin in the center and then proceed outward to the outer edges.

The Amish women often quilt in this way. Their simple but forceful use of geometric designs and the placement of intense solid colors side by side are impressive. Although the piecing of these quilts is simple, the quilting isn't. Each is embellished with elaborate designs made in tiny precise stitches. Roses, tulips, feathers, wreaths, diamonds, and stars are favorite designs.

No one is quite sure when the Amish began making this type of quilt. It is generally thought that it wasn't until the middle of the nineteenth century, with most of the quilts in the traditional patterns being constructed between 1870 and 1935.

Three shapes are used primarily for the Amish quilts—the square, triangle, and rectangle. As the families moved to other localities, variations in the placement of the shapes seem to have appeared in the designs.

Some of the typical quilt designs are shown here. Although they may seem very simple, try to imagine how they will look when thousands of tiny stitches hold the layers together.

 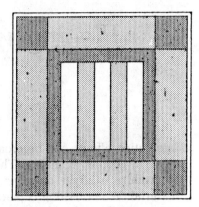

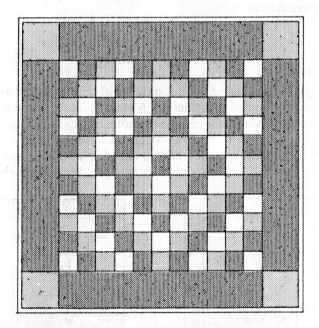

10

Piecing with Strips

Interesting effects can be created by using strips of fabric instead of geometric shapes. The strips can be seamed together to produce a larger piece or sewn one by one to a backing material. When batting is placed between the backing and the strips a puffy quilted look results. This is an easy way to gain attractive results.

Pressed Piecing

This type of piecing offers not only a different look but also a different method of construction. A strip of fabric is sewn to a backing and then pressed before another strip is added. This procedure is often referred to as pressed piecing. It is a technique that works nicely when assembling strip designs that may be hundreds of years old. Some of the designs are shown

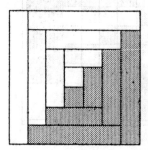
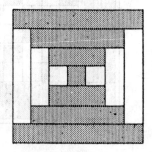

here. The piecing begins at the center of the block with the work progressing outward to the edges. The piecing can be done by hand or machine. Pressed piecing makes it possible to insert a layer of batting between the backing and top, and to hold it in place with the stitches that secure the strips.

It is wise to plan the design you want to make on graph paper, indicating the color scheme with fabric swatches. In this way you will know the placement of each color.

LOG CABIN DESIGN

For this design you will need two templates—one for the backing or foundation, which is usually made of muslin, and the second for the center square. The template for the backing should be 1/2 inch (1.3 cm) larger on each side than the finished block. For example, a 10 1/2-inch (26.8-cm) block will be made on an 11 1/2-inch (29.3-cm) square. The size of the center template depends on the width of the strips. For instance, if the finished strips will be 1 1/2 inches (3.8 cm) wide, they will be cut 2 inches (5 cm) wide in order to allow for seam allowances. The center square will therefore be cut 2 inches by 2 inches (5 cm by 5 cm) so when sewn it will be 1 1/2 inches by 1 1/2 inches (3.8 cm by 3.8 cm).

Templates are not needed to cut the fabric strips. They can be cut on the lengthwise grain of the material and of any length. Strips 18 inches (46 cm) long are easy to handle when working on a small project. This makes it unnecessary to purchase more fabrics than you need just to get a long strip. The number of strips you need will depend on your design.

Cutting the Strips. Before cutting the strips, draw a straight line parallel to the selvage. Cut along this line, discarding the selvage edge. In order to establish a guide for stitching, mark the width of the seam allowance on both sides. For example, for a 1-inch (2.5-cm) strip, measure from 1/4 inch (6 mm) and mark, then 1 inch (2.5 cm), and finally another 1/4 inch (6 mm). Mark at intervals the length of the fabric, connecting them with drawn lines. Cut carefully on these lines.

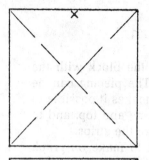

Backing. On the backing, draw diagonal lines from corner to corner. This marks the center of the block. Also mark the top of the block with an X.

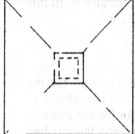

Center. Cut a square the width of the strips. Place it on the backing with the right side up. Match the corners with the diagonal lines. Baste in place.

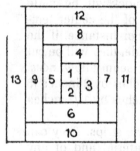

Before beginning to piece, study the diagram shown here. It will give you some idea as to how the strips are arranged and the order of sewing. Although the work is done counterclockwise, it could be done clockwise.

Sewing. Begin by pinning the correct strip over the center square. The right sides should be together and the seam lines matching. Cut the strip exactly the same length as the square. If you are sewing by hand use running stitches, making sure that the stitches penetrate the backing. The work can be done by machine. Sew carefully so the seam allowances will be even at all times. Turn the strip to the right side and press it flat.

Pin the second strip in position along the two pieces that have just been sewn together. Cut the strip, which will be twice the length of the first one. Sew in place and press.

Continue in this way until the block is completed. Watch carefully so the strips are cut the correct length, using the pieces already sewn as a guide, and always press after each one is sewn in place.

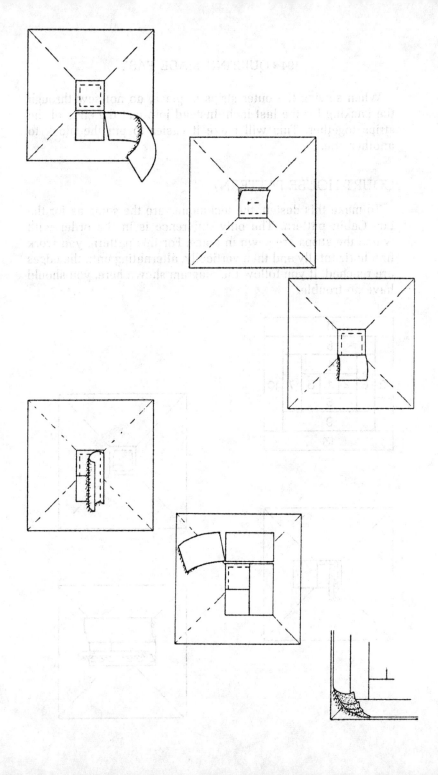

When sewing the outer strips in place, do not sew through the backing for the last inch. Instead join just the ends of the strips together. This will make it easier to pin the block to another one.

COURT HOUSE PATTERN

To make this design, the techniques are the same as for the Log Cabin pattern. The only difference is in the order with which the strips are sewn in place. For this pattern, you work first horizontally and then vertically, alternating until the edges are reached. If you follow the diagram shown here, you should have no trouble.

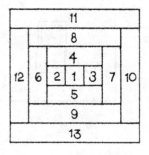

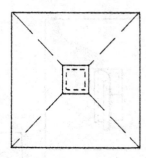

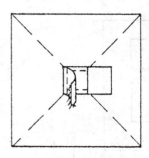

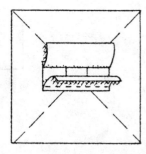

Strip Piecing

If you are looking for a quick and easy way to put fabric together to create interesting geometric patterns, then strip piecing is for you. Much of the tedious work is eliminated. Geometric patterns appear as if by magic.

Strip piecing can be done in different ways. In one method, the strips are sewn to a backing as when making a Log Cabin block. In another, the strips are joined to create a wider strip from which smaller pieces are cut and then put together to produce a limitless number of fascinating designs. This is the method used for Seminole-Type patchwork (see page 198).

PREPARING THE STRIPS

Begin as always with a design in mind and how it is to be used. The designs are adaptable. They work as nicely for clothing as they do for quilts.

Materials. While other types of piecing can usually be done with small bits of fabric, strip piecing needs larger ones from which longer strips can be cut.

A 100 percent cotton is the favorite. It seems to be the easiest to handle. The seams are smooth and clearly defined after pressing. The fabric ravels little, an important consideration when working with narrow strips.

If care is a problem, then a blend of cotton and polyester will prove more satisfactory. Be sure that it doesn't ravel or feel limp. Both characteristics can create problems, especially when sewing a soft fabric to a firm cotton one. A soft fabric is more difficult to cut and stitch.

Both types of fabric should be fairly closely woven and on grain. Materials such as broadcloth, calico, muslin, and percale, in a weight commonly used for blouses, work well.

A washable fabric should be washed before it is cut. You want to be sure that the material will not shrink after the article is made and that it is colorfast. Iron it carefully, following the lengthwise grain of the fabric. Do not wiggle the iron. The fabrics will not lie smooth if you do.

Backing. If you are using the Log Cabin method, you will need some backing material such as muslin. A sheet also works well. Batting too can be used.

Thread. Cotton or cotton-covered polyester thread can be used. Cotton is often thought to be best for cotton fabrics, cotton-covered polyester for blends. Whichever produces the best effect is the one to use.

Cutting. Begin by pressing the fabric. Place it on a firm surface with the wrong side up and smooth it out. Draw a straight line the length of the material 1/4 inch (6 mm) from the selvage. The selvage should not be part of a strip. From this line the width of the strips will be established. Only the cutting line needs to be marked, so be sure to include the 1/4-inch (6-mm) seam allowance when deciding how wide to cut the strips. For instance, if your design plan calls for a 1-inch (2.5-cm) strip, you will mark it 1 1/2 inches (3.8 cm) wide. Mark the cutting lines. Use a yardstick or transparent ruler. You want to be sure each line is accurately marked and cut. Cutting the strips on the lengthwise grain makes it easier to measure and cut them with precision. Also there is less stretch when working with the lengthwise rather than the crosswise grain.

STRIPS WITH BACKING

This is one of the methods you can use. It doesn't allow for a great variety of designs, but it is very easy to do. Sometimes when the strips are cut very narrow, it is called string quilting. Although strips follow a straight direction parallel to each other, the strips can be angled to produce diagonal effects. There are no limitations on the number of fabrics that can be used or the width of the strips.

With the strips cut the correct width and the foundation cut to the size and shape of the finished piece, place the piece wrong side up on a firm surface. If you wish, you can place a layer of batting on it.

Pin the first strip across the top with the right side up. Baste along the outside edges, joining the three layers together. (A)

Place the second strip on top of the first strip with the right sides together. Pin in place. Then stitch the two strips together,

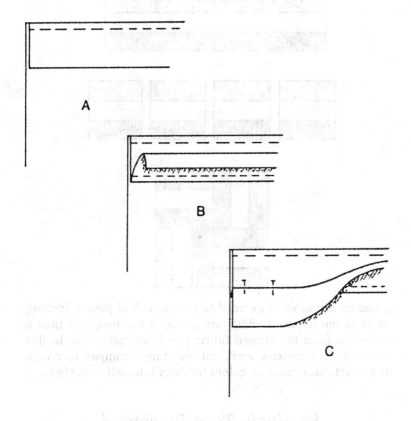

leaving a 1/4-inch (6-mm) seam allowance. The stitching penetrates the layers of batting and backing. (B)

Turn the second strip to the right side. Smooth it out and pin
in place. (C) Attach the third strip in the same way as the
second. Continue in this way until the backing piece is covered
with strips.

If the strips extend beyond the side edges, turn the piece to
the wrong side. Trim the strips even with the backing.

STRIPS WITHOUT BACKING

Sometimes strip piecing can duplicate certain patchwork designs. For example, for the Roman Stripes shown here, tem-

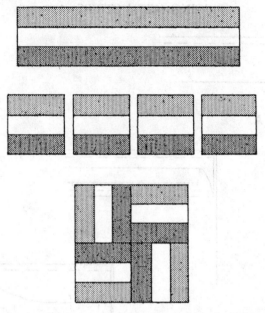

plates do not have to be used to cut individual pieces. Instead strips of the required width can be sewn together, and then a shape cut from the striped fabric you have just made. In this instance, four squares were cut and then arranged to create this effect. Variations in colors produce interesting designs.

Seminole-Type Patchwork

The Seminole Indians created this type of strip piecing. The dramatic and intricate designs were used for their pieced fashions.

To create the various effects, the strips of material in varying widths are sewn together by machine. The finished strip is then cut into rectangles, squares, rhomboids, or triangles. Of course, if you wish, you can use just a ruler and pencil. Draw the outline of the piece directly on the wrong side of the fabric, measuring each section accurately. The rectangle is the easiest shape to work with.

After sewing the strips together, press them open. Then mark the fabric, remembering to leave a seam allowance. Cut the

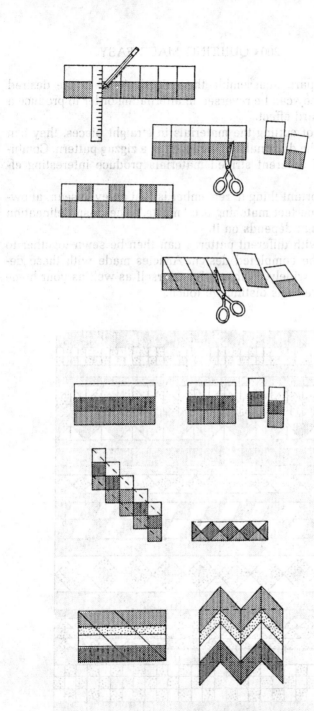

sections apart. Reassemble the striped pieces in the desired pattern. They can be reversed in alternating order to produce a checkerboard effect.

Instead of cutting the materials in straight pieces, they can be cut on the diagonal and arranged in a zigzag pattern. Combinations of different striped materials produce interesting effects.

An important thing to remember is that an even seam allowance and perfect matching are "musts." The crisp delineation of the design depends on it.

Bands with different patterns can then be sewn together to produce the completed design. Articles made with these designs vary widely. Fashions for yourself as well as your home can be given this distinctive touch.

11

Tops Without Quilting

Quilts and quilting material can be made without using any tiny quilting stitches. In fact some of the most unusual and attractive designs are made this way. Two ways of creating these effects are mentioned here.

Crazy Patchwork

Of all of the types of patchwork, many feel that this is the most fun to make. The tedious task of cutting out the same shape is eliminated. Sewing the pieces together with precision is forgotten. You can work with abandon. In fact you can do your own thing. Pieces can be placed in random fashion to create a lovely collage of color and texture.

Although the crazy quilt was probably born of necessity, it became a fad in the Victorian period. No home was complete without one, not to be used as a quilt but instead as a throw for the parlor. Draped over the end of a sofa, it added a decorative touch. The pieces were garnered from many unlikely places, but usually each one brought back a memory. Often family members and friends supplied the pieces and often the scraps were used just as they were received. A baby's dress, a man's tie, a graduation ribbon, a prize winner's badge, a friend's wedding dress might be the source of the patch. Some of the quilts were made of silk and velvet, others of calico and wool.

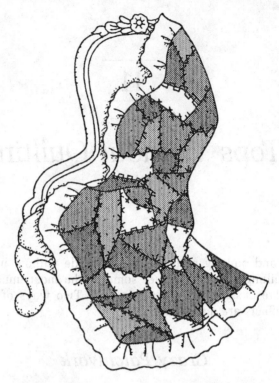

To this mélange, embroidery stitches were added. In fact the pieces were often held in place with fancy stitches covering the edges. The more adept one was with the needle, the more intricate the embroidery. Often the finished article was judged not by the pleasing arrangement of textures and colors but by the originality of the stitches.

Each crazy patchwork is one-of-a-kind—there can obviously be no duplicates.

Although the original crazy quilts should not be considered quilting in the true sense, contemporary crazy quilting can be. The early quilts were made without a layer of batting. This has been added to the crazy patchwork of today.

MATERIALS

Today, patchwork can be done by machine. This makes it quicker and easier to do. Instead of folding under the edges as you do when sewing by hand, overlapping and seaming handle this procedure nicely. Crazy patchwork is used for a variety of decorative articles, ranging from an eyeglass case to a wall hanging. The all-over effect seems to create a very contemporary look.

For the Top. For this type of patchwork, you do not have to make a separate decorative top. Instead you pin the three layers together as you sew the pieces in place. The pieces are placed on top of the batting and the backing.

As in the making of any piece of needlework, it is best to make a few plans. Although the ones for crazy patchwork aren't as specific as in other cases, the results will be more pleasing if you have some idea as to the color scheme and the types of fabric.

Today one doesn't always have a ragbag as Grandmother did. You will probably have to buy new fabrics. Of course the type you purchase will depend on what you have decided to make. You may need materials that are easy to care for and relatively durable, or you may feel that you can use more elegant fabrics. If cleaning is a consideration and if the article is to be laundered, be sure that the materials are preshrunk and colorfast.

Variety in the fabrics is not limited. However, too many different ones can spoil the look of unity in the finished piece. Often combining printed and solid fabrics offers an interesting look. Small prints are easier to handle and more effective than large ones. In planning the over-all effect, remember that embroidery stitches are more distinctive on plain fabrics. This should influence the positioning of the printed and solid pieces. Be sure to press the fabric before you start to sew.

For the Backing. The material you use will depend on the project you are making and the effect you want. Usually a cotton fabric, such as muslin or a sheet, works well. For a stiffer effect, try a nonwoven interfacing. A lightweight cotton lining material will be better for a softer look.

For the Inner Layer. Although it isn't necessary to use a layer of batting, it does add warmth and a protective padding, making it possible to use the resulting fabric for a wide variety of articles. The batting seems to add a pleasing textural quality.

Polyester batting seems best, with the bonded variety easiest to cut and work with. The weight of the batting you select depends on what you are making and how puffy you want the article to look. Experiment by using multiple layers of the lightweight type. This will give you some idea as to the effect each will give. Usually it is wise to decrease the weight as the weight of the fabric increases. A lightweight one works well for clothing, a medium-weight for something like a place mat, and a heavyweight for a quilt.

SHAPES

There are no rules to guide you in selecting the shapes of the pieces. Only your eyes and artistic sense will insure a pleasing effect. Some people use squares and rectangles sparingly, preferring triangles and the more unusual shapes such as the rhomboid and trapezoid. To relieve the angularity of the design, some curves can be added, although it is impossible to sew the pieces in place by machine. If large pieces are used, the work can be done more quickly, but smaller ones will create a more pleasing pattern.

If your fabric is in a large piece, you may want to cut it into smaller strips, about 6 to 8 inches (15 to 20.5 cm) in width. This makes the material easier to handle. Scraps of fabric can be left in their original form.

SEWING

Experimenting is also a good practice when there are no specific rules to follow in sewing. In this way, you get a feel for developing a design as you sew.

By Machine. Cut a piece for the backing the required size and shape. A square will be easy to handle.

To the backing piece add one of batting. Baste the two together along the edges.

For the top piece, cut the fabric in the desired shape, one that will fit into a corner. Pin it in place. If you begin in the upper left-hand corner, you can progress to the lower right-hand corner.

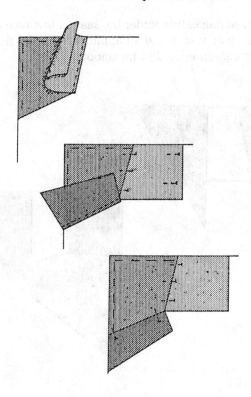

The shape of the next piece can be determined before it is stitched or cut after it is sewed in place. Put this piece on the first one, right sides together, along one side of the first piece. Stitch a 1/4-inch (6-mm) seam, joining the two pieces. Separate the two pieces, bringing the second piece over the batting. Cut to the desired shape. Smooth out the piece but do not press it. Pin in place so it won't move as the next piece is sewn in position.

Add the third piece in the same way. It can be placed on either side of the first piece in order to create the correct effect. Continue to work in this way until the square is completely covered.

For a curved piece, turn under the seam allowance and apply it right side up as you would an appliqué. Clip the seam allowance so the curved edge will lie smooth.

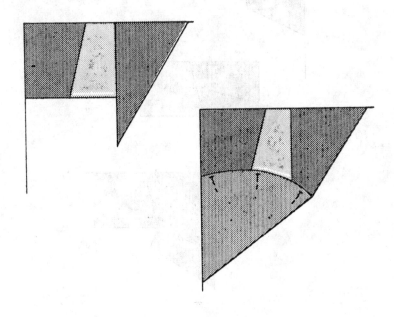

When *joining light and dark fabrics,* be careful that a dark seam allowance does not show through the lighter one. Trimming the darker seam allowance will be helpful.

If you find the pieces have formed a right angle, don't try to add a square. It will be difficult to stitch. Instead apply a curving piece. You could decide to change the design slightly by stitching a piece to one side of the square, extending it across the other side, forming a straight seam. The excess fabric can be cut away.

When all pieces are in place, baste around the edges. You are now ready to start embroidering.

By Hand. If you decide to work by hand, assemble the backing square as you did for machine sewing. Place the first piece in the corner, right side up, and baste in place.

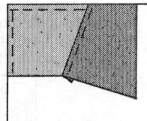

For the second piece, which is cut in the correct shape, including a 1/4-inch (6-mm) seam allowance, turn under the edge that is to be placed over the first piece. Position it, right side up, lapping it over the first piece, matching seam allowances. Baste in place.

Continue to add pieces in this way, folding under any edge that will be exposed when the block is completed.

When all pieces are basted in place, sew each folded edge. This can be done with sewing or embroidery stitches. Of course the embroidery stitches will produce a more decorative

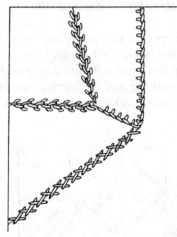

effect and are the ones most often seen on a crazy quilt. Any stitch that spans both sides of the seam line, such as the feather, herringbone, or blanket, will be functional and decorative.

If you just want to sew the pieces in place, you can do that with a slip or blind hemming stitch. Take very tiny stitches so they will be almost invisible.

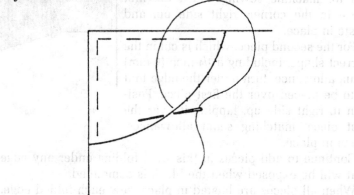

Cathedral Windows

Among traditional designs, Cathedral Windows is unique. The stained-glass look is lovely and intriguing. How it is made is a puzzle. It is difficult to decipher how the diamond-in-circle design is produced. No quilting and no batting are needed. Raw edges are concealed. Even stitches are hard to find. The three--

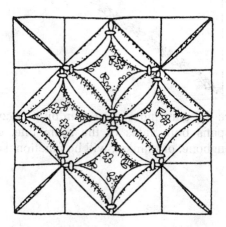

dimensional effect just seems to happen. In fact, folding is more of a contributing factor than stitching.

Variations in color and size are many. Although the background is usually thought of as being light in color, it really doesn't have to be. A fascinating quilt in a recent national exhibit had a darkened foundation in blue with golden windows worked in different hues and values to create a rich sculptural surface.

As for size, it, too, can vary. Usually the pattern begins with squares, 7 to 9 inches (18 to 23 cm). In deciding on the dimensions, keep in mind the size of the article you are making. The resulting squares should be kept in proportion to the over-all size. When making your decision, remember that the final square is only about one half the size of the original one.

MATERIALS

For the foundation, unbleached muslin is the fabric most often used, although others can be substituted. Lovely effects can be created when lights and darks or plain and patterned fabrics are interchanged. Cottons in the same weight as the muslin handle nicely. Be sure that it is woven on grain. This will make it easier to fold the piece neatly.

For the windows, the same type of fabric is used. Usually it is in a contrasting color, either plain or patterned. The designs should be small for the best effect.

Although batting is not used in the construction of the traditional design, it is sometimes tucked under the window. This adds a certain puffiness to the design.

For the thread, use regular sewing thread. Matching thread will produce the best effect.

TOOLS

No special equipment is needed. For the measuring and marking, a pencil and ruler are sufficient for making cardboard templates.

Sewing needles, straight pins, and scissors complete the sewing needs.

CONSTRUCTION

One of the advantages of using Cathedral Windows for a top is the ease with which each piece is handled. A square can be tucked in your bag to be done when you have a little time for sewing. It is amazing how quickly the number of squares will increase.

Because of the unusual nature of the construction, it is best to start with a practice piece. In this way, the puzzle will be solved. You will understand how folding and a few stitches produce a unique design. The stitches can be made by hand or machine.

Cutting. Three squares are needed. Two are larger than the other one. Marking the cloth will be helpful.

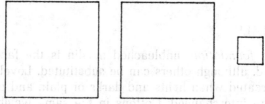

For the larger squares, cut two pieces 8 inches (20.3 cm) square. Accuracy is a "must." Unless the squares are cut on the grain, you will not be able to fold the fabric, so it is important that the folded edges be on a true bias.

For the smaller square, which is the window, cut a piece 2¼ inches (5.1 cm) square.

Sewing. Begin by folding a larger square in half with the right sides together. Sew a ¼-inch (6-mm) seam along the short ends. This can be done by machine or by hand. Keep the stitches small. Be sure the seam allowance is even. Press the rectangle.

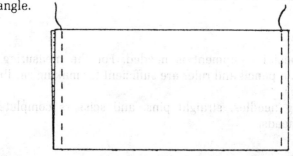

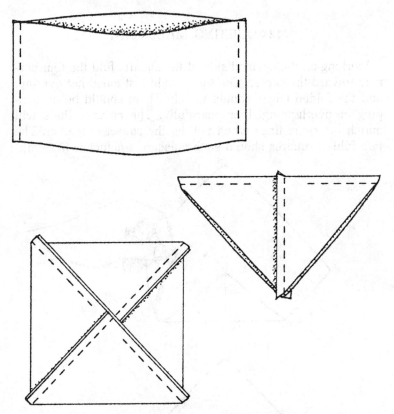

Open the rectangle, bringing the seams together. As you do this, the piece seems to fall into a triangle. Match the raw edges, sew a 1/4-inch (6-mm) seam across the top, starting from the corners and leaving an opening of 1 1/2 inches (3.8 cm) in the center. Press the seams to one side, not open. Note that the seamed ends and open edges form an X across the square. Clip the extra material at the corners.

Turn the rectangle to the right side. Flatten it into a square. Fold under the edges of the opening so they just meet and the stitched seams fall on the fold lines. Be sure the corners are square. Press flat.

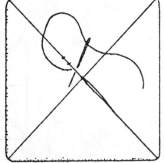

Close the opening with tiny overhand stitches and press flat. The square should now measure about 5 1/4 inches (13.3 cm).

Working on the seamed side of the square, fold the four corners toward the center. The tips should just meet, not overlap, and the folded edges should match. There should be no gapping or overlapping. Press carefully. The creased lines will match the seam lines when putting the squares together. The two folded squares should each measure 3⁵/₈ inches (9.2 cm).

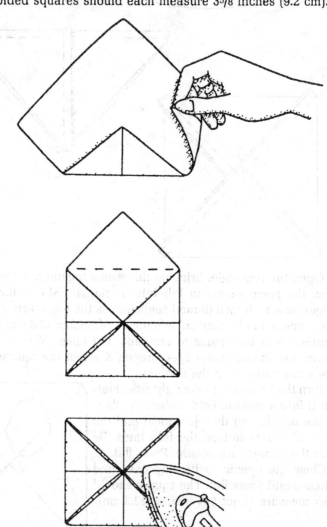

Place the two blocks side by side with the pointed sections up. Working with the flaps that touch, pick up one from each block. Pin them together along the creased seam lines. Sew the two together by hand or machine. Machine stitching produces a stronger piece. Stitch exactly on the line, back-tacking at each end, duplicating the stitching line exactly. Press flaps down into their original positions and tack in place.

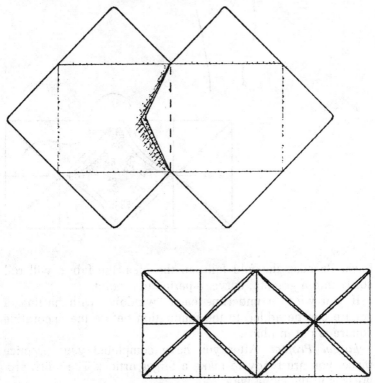

The Window. The window is placed over the seam line. Cut a piece of contrasting fabric 2¼ inches (5.7 cm) square. Lay it on top of a triangular flap on each block, creating a diamond shape.

To conceal the raw edges, turn the four folded edges over it. Sew the folded edge in place with invisible hand stitches. The stitches must pass through all the layers of fabric, including the

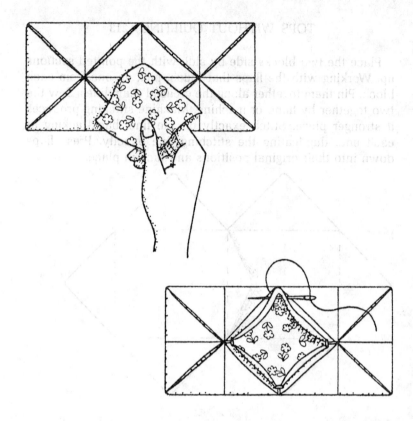

back. Because the fold falls on the bias, the fabric will roll softly into a graceful curve, tapering to a point.

If you wish to underline each "window" with batting, a square can be added to the foundation before the decorative square is put in place.

Larger Project. After you have completed your practice piece, you are ready to make a larger article. The work progresses in the same way.

Be sure that each square, large and small, is cut the same size and on grain. A template for each size will help to keep the marking and cutting accurate. Make as many blocks as you need for the project. When the work is completed, you will notice that the folding seems to create small petallike shapes and an interlocking diamond-in-circle design.

12

Embroidery and Quilting

If you attend exhibits and auctions of antique and contemporary quilts you know that sometimes you will find one that does not fall into any of the categories that have already been mentioned. Often decorative touches are added. Unusual combinations of fabrics, colors, and shapes make traditional designs seem different. Among these is the embroidered top.

Embroidered Designs

Although today simple embroidery seems to be used only for designs for children, there was a time when the "workt" or embroidered spread was held in high esteem. Embroidery probably first appeared on quilts as a decorative way of prolonging the life of the fabric. Worn spots were covered with decorative stitches. Gradually more and more areas were covered with embroidery until, at last, fancy stitches embellished the surface in a planned fashion. Embroidery was sometimes used alone, as in crewel work, and at others to outline patches as we do appliqués today with chain, stem, and buttonhole stitches.

About 1850 embroidery on wool became popular and continued through the Victorian period. A quilt of this type was often referred to as a blanket. Sometimes the blanket was handwoven in a check pattern, representative of a quilt block, with red

and blue threads forming the checks. A floral design was then embroidered in each square.

Another design might have embroidered strips applied to a quilted background. Occasionally the squares created the effect of tiles, with the embroidery in black or dark blue on a light background.

The stitches most often seen on the older quilts are easy-to-work ones. They include outline or stem, cross, seed, satin, buttonhole, feather, French knot, split, and flat stitches. Delicate airy effects could be created by some of them and solid, heavier motifs by others. Arranging them in attractive designs taxed the artistic ability of the embroiderer. When you remember that a woman had to draw her own pattern, decide what colors to use, where to place them, and then proceed to create the embroidery in her favorite stitches, you are amazed at the beauty of the finished article.

Designs often depicted real people and animals. It might be the parson, a bluebird, wild flowers growing in the fields. Intertwining flowers and vines, leaves and scrolls were favorites. Tuliplike flowers were popular with the Dutch ladies on Long

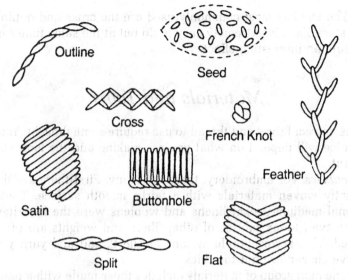

Outline

Seed

Cross

French Knot

Satin

Buttonhole

Feather

Split

Flat

Island and the Germans in Pennsylvania. The feather crest of the Prince of Wales was frequently used as a background for a floral arrangement in New England, Maryland, and Virginia. Sometimes the flower or leaf took on a geometric-type form. Usually open space was left around the motif, creating a feeling of freedom.

Homespun, woven of linen or wool, was the fabric most often used. Sometimes cotton was added. This produced a texture that sometimes was rather coarse. However, the effect of the stitches on it created an interesting look.

Today, only simple forms of embroidery are used. Perhaps someday more elaborate embroidery will again be in fashion. Until then, use touches to enhance a surface and create added interest, such as when appliqué or crazy piecing is the dominant feature. Or decorate blocks with pictorial designs that may amuse a child or portray your fondness for something, such as butterflies. Recently a quilt was made from blue jeans, with each block embroidered to illustrate an experience in the life of a young woman. Easy-to-make stitches can be used, employing fascinating colors. Working on small pieces of material makes the project simple to handle and quick to do.

The stitches most commonly used are the cross and outline or stem. Each is extremely easy to do but at the same time can create an interesting effect.

Materials and Tools

The correct fabric and thread to use require some thought. Your choice will depend on what you are making and the look you want.

Fabrics. For embroidery, there are many. First there are the tightly woven materials with a fairly smooth surface. Traditional medium-weight linens and woolens were the favorites. However, today fabrics of other fibers and weights are often used. This is acceptable as long as the thread and yarn you have chosen are not too thick.

The next group of materials includes those made with a plain weave, with the same number of threads per inch (2.5 cm) moving lengthwise and crosswise. The evenness of the threads is a distinguishing characteristic, allowing it to be used for thread-counting techniques, such as cross stitch and hemstitching. The fabric can be fine or coarse, ranging from 36 threads to 14 per inch (2.5 cm). Sometimes groups of threads are interwoven, such as for Aida and Hardanger cloths. You will find this type of fabric made of cotton, linen, wool, synthetics, and blends of these.

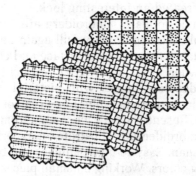

Then there are fabrics with surface interest, such as gingham. The evenly spaced pattern creates a grid that provides guidelines to follow. The design can be printed or woven. Whichever method has been used, you should be sure that the pattern follows the grain line. Printing off grain will upset the appearance of the stitches. Cross stitching can be worked most effectively on this type of material.

Thread. The type you select depends on the stitch you are using and the effect you want. Although there are many from which to choose, embroidery floss and pearl cotton will probably work best.

Cotton floss is a favorite. It is available in a wide range of colors. The floss is a loosely twisted thread in six strands that may be separated. This allows you to use a finer thread for finer work. Floss is also made in silk and rayon.

Pearl cotton has a twisted texture and a high sheen. It is a two-ply thread and comes in different sizes—8, 5, and 3, the heaviest.

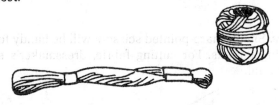

Experiment with other threads and yarns if you wish. New ones are constantly appearing and may create the effect you are looking for. The main thing to remember is that there should be compatibility between the thread and the fabric.

TOOLS

Not many pieces of equipment are needed, but those that are should be carefully selected. The beauty of the work often depends on the correct coordination of needle, thread, and fabric.

Embroidery Hoop. This is a "must" for working on small pieces of material. It holds the fabric flat and smooth so the stitches can be easily made. Hoops are available in various sizes and shapes. A hand-held one in diameters of 4 to 12

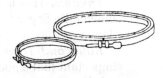

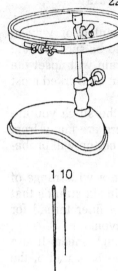

1 10

inches (10 to 30.5 cm) is the most portable. The hoop is sometimes attached to a standard, which you can set on the floor, chair, or table so that both of your hands are free to handle the embroidery. Always choose the one that is most convenient to use and best for the work you are doing.

Needles. There are different kinds of needles. The one you will find most suitable for this type of embroidery is the crewel. Its sharp point and long, slender eye allows it to accommodate the thread nicely and to penetrate the fabric easily.

Scissors. Small, sharp-pointed scissors will be handy to have for snipping threads. For cutting fabric, dressmaker's shears will be helpful.

Thimble. This is a most important protective tool. It allows the middle finger to push the needle through the fabric without damage.

Ruler and Tape Measure. Accurate measurements are so important that a good flexible tape measure and straight-edged ruler are necessary.

MOTIF

Now is the time for you to decide whether you want to create a design of your own or use one that you have seen in a book or magazine. Don't be afraid to test your creative ability. You can be sure it will give you great satisfaction.

Designing. Of course it will be easier if you purchase a pattern that is ready to be transferred to the fabric. In case you can't find exactly the pattern you want, then try adapting a design from a greeting card, scarf, wallpaper, china, or some other decorative piece. When you have decided on a design you like, cover it with tracing paper and carefully trace the outline. Keep in mind that you are going to interpret it in embroidery stitches, not copy it exactly. This will probably simplify the design considerably.

Color. As soon as you have decided on the design, it is time to think about color. The color you select will influence the mood. To be sure you have an idea as to how the finished piece will look, it is a good idea to make a color plan. Color the traced design. You may need to try several color schemes before you get exactly what you want.

SIZING THE DESIGN

If the design you have chosen isn't the correct size, you can change it without too much trouble. This can be done commercially (at a place that photocopies, usually) or you can make the alteration yourself. Having the original art photostated to your specifications will be easier and not too expensive. However, if this isn't a possibility, you can use the grid system to transpose the design to graph paper with larger or smaller squares. Directions for increasing and decreasing the size of a design are discussed in Chapter 8.

In planning the design, remember that there is an upper and lower edge to it as well as a right- and left-hand side. Not recognizing this fact may lead you to prepare a design that moves in an opposite direction from the one you had planned for. You don't want a design going backward when it should move forward.

Transferring Designs

There are several ways to transfer a design to fabric. Of course it will depend on how the motif was prepared.

Hot-Iron Transfer. The design has been printed on a heat-sensitive paper. When the motif is placed on the fabric and touched by an iron, the transfer is made. Read carefully the directions that accompany the commercially made pattern. You want to be sure the temperature of the iron is correct.

Before you begin, cut away any part of the design as well as lettering that you do not need. Because temperature is so important, test it with a piece of the discarded lettering. When you are sure the temperature is all right, place the transfer design face down on the fabric.

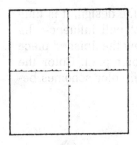

To position the design correctly, you may want to fold the piece into quarters and press lightly, establishing crease lines. Also fold the pattern in the same way, making sure that the design is centered. Open the pattern carefully, placing it over the fabric with the fold lines of the pattern matching the crease lines of the fabric. Pin the transfer in place at corners.

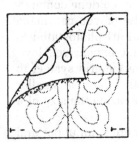

Apply the iron according to directions. Raise and lower the iron as you change its position. Do not shove it around. To make sure that the transferring of the design is taking place, inspect it before removing the pattern. Lift just a corner of it. If the impression needs to be clearer, reapply the iron.

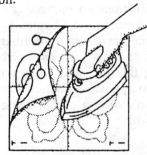

To make an original hot-iron transfer, use a special transfer pencil. On a piece of heavy tracing paper, copy the design. Turn paper over. Using the transfer pencil, draw over lines on the back.

Then place the marked side down on the material. Anchor it in place with pins. Press with the iron as for a commercial pattern.

Dressmaker's Carbon. Used with a tracing wheel, this offers another way to transfer a design. Place the design right side up on the fabric. Pin three corners securely in place. Slip a piece of carbon paper carefully under it with carbon side down. Using a tracing wheel, draw over the design lines. If you have trouble controlling the tracing wheel you might find a pencil or a knitting needle easier to handle.

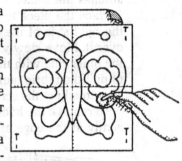

Pricking the Design. Although this is an old-fashioned way of marking, it is still a reliable method. In Chapter 6 this manner of transferring a design is discussed more fully (see page 105). Patterns of this type can be purchased or you can make them yourself by pricking the design pattern with small holes. A fine powder is then dusted over the holes, leaving the outline on the fabric when the pattern is removed—carefully, to avoid smudging. If necessary, use a sharp pencil to make the design more distinct by connecting the dots.

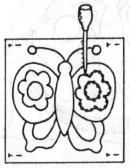

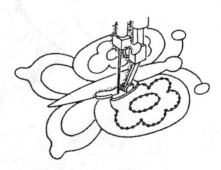

Embroidery Techniques

With the design carefully transferred to the fabric, you are ready to start the embroidery. This is always fun. Watching a simple design come alive by simply using a needle and thread creates a feeling of satisfaction.

Using a Hoop. This is important. It holds the material taut during the embroidery process, allowing you to keep the stitches the same.

Place the piece to be embroidered over the inner hoop with the right side of the design up. Slip the outer part of the hoop over it. Move slowly around the hoop, pushing down gently on the outer ring with the heel of your hand. At the same time, try to pull the fabric taut with thumb and fingers. It may be necessary to adjust the screw on the outer ring so it fits more snugly.

To remove the hoop, press the material and inner hoop down gently at the edge of the hoop with your thumbs.

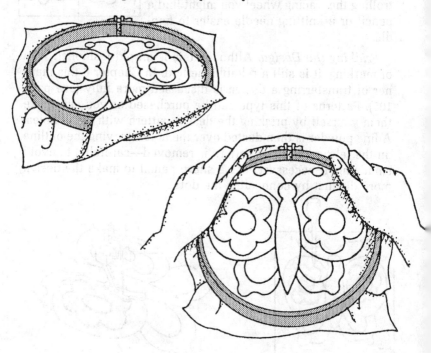

Stem Stitch. This easy-to-do stitch is used primarily to outline designs. The solid line it forms defines a drawing nicely. Animals, birds, flowers, and objects of interest can take on a realistic look. When used for a coverlet or quilt, the embroidered blocks have an educational value as well as an artistic one. I remember how much fun it was, as a little girl, to look through a box of design squares at the store. Finding a picture you just loved was a moment of pleasure. Often family and friends embroidered the blocks, so the finished product was something to be recalled with affection. Years ago many a little girl took her first embroidery stitch on one of these blocks.

The stitches were often made in a bright color so the design stood out in bold relief against a white background. Keeping the stitches small and even produces a more definite line.

Assembling the blocks is done after all have been embroidered. Arrange them in a pleasing design and then decide how to join them for the correct size. This can be done in various ways. Sometimes they are set together, side by side; at others, with plain blocks between. The embroidered designs always seem to appear more attractive when they are set off with the plain blocks.

Quilting stitches add another decorative touch. This can be done on each block before they are set together or after they have all been joined. The quilting stitches usually follow a straight line, moving vertically, horizontally, or diagonally.

Cross Stitch. Designs much more intricate in detail can be embroidered with cross stitches. Shading with a variety of colors produces a three-dimensional effect, giving character to the designs. A menagerie of animals can come alive. The family tree can be preserved forever. Or it may be local buildings or events that will be remembered this way. The solid effect that the stitches produce when massed together makes this all possible.

Patterns are available in magazines or, if you wish, you can purchase them as hot-iron transfers or as charted designs to be copied on even-weave fabric or canvas.

With even-weave fabrics on which the groups of thread can easily be counted, it may not be necessary to transfer the design to fabric. Instead you can count the threads as you cross stitch. With counted-thread fabric, the threads form a natural

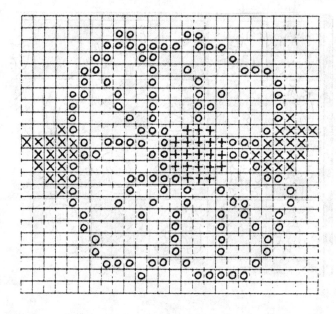

grid over which the stitches can be made. A stitch can cover a one-thread intersection or several, depending on the coarseness of the weave and the size of the stitch desired.

The charted design may be in color, showing exactly where the different colors are to be placed. Sometimes this type of design is printed in black and white with symbols denoting where the colors are to be placed and the colors to be used.

In making the stitches, be sure that each stitch crosses the other stitch in the same direction, and that it crosses the same number of fabric threads. This consistency is most important.

With gingham, another fabric that provides a nice background for charted cross stitches, you count squares, not threads. However, it is most important that the fabric be woven on grain in order for the rows of stitches to remain straight and the design balanced. The checks make the necessary grid, with one cross being made within each square. This keeps the stitches uniform in size.

Gingham is available in various check sizes from 3 to 10 per inch (2.5 cm). Since the size of the checks controls the size of each stitch, the smaller the squares, the smaller the completed design will be. Be sure in planning your design that you consider this feature when using gingham.

For plain fabrics in which the threads or designs cannot be counted, transfer the designs to the fabric. A hot-iron transfer will be the easiest to use.

The completed blocks can be assembled and joined in a variety of ways. Use the set and frame that seem to create the most interesting effect.

When your design is finished, you are then ready to follow the directions in Chapter 6.

13

Stenciling for Color

If you are searching for a different look, you might try painting. The effect resembles an appliqué and is much quicker to do. Recently fiber-reactive dyes and fabric paints have become available. There are even wax crayons to use. If this type of embellishment interests you, check the various products in art supply stores. Also look at the stencils. They provide an interesting way for adding color to a surface.

Today stenciling is having a popular revival. Its place in history goes back centuries. The Chinese and Japanese decorated their clothing with stenciled designs. In the Middle Ages the Europeans decorated church walls and religious articles. The French used stencils to color wallpaper by the end of the seventeenth century. In colonial America, walls and furniture were given this attractive touch. Later the designs were applied to fabric.

Between 1820 and 1840 the stenciled spread became popular and prized for its beauty. The stenciled quilt seems to have been created more as a decorative piece than as a functional one.

Stenciled quilts of that period are rare to find except in museums. However, when you find one, it is lavish with blossoms and buds intertwined with stems and leaves. An open rose was a popular motif. Sometimes patchwork was used with stenciled blocks. Often beautiful quilting enhanced the stenciled design to create a very fine spread.

Supplies to Use

Stenciling is a way of applying color to a surface through the use of a precisely cut pattern. Although you can cut your own stencil, there is a wide variety of designs to be purchased. It is also possible to buy commercial patterns that show you how and where to use a stencil. Be sure to read the directions very carefully to ensure good results. It is always wise to experiment before you stencil the actual fabric.

Fabric. The material should be clean, dry, and free of wrinkles before placing the stencil on it. Stretch the fabric taut as you anchor it to a board. Be sure to position the design carefully. Once the paint is applied, it is impossible to change it. Let the material dry thoroughly before finishing the project.

Brushes. There are brushes especially made for stenciling. The applicator is round and has a blunt end. Brushes are available in a variety of sizes.

Always begin with a clean dry brush. If you are using several colors you will need several brushes. It is time-consuming to wash and dry a brush before starting a different color.

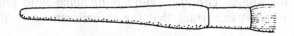

Paint. Various types of paints are available. Acrylic ones are often recommended. Available in a wide variety of colors, they can be used just as they come from the tube. The consistency seems just right for making sharp edges. Also they dry quickly and can be washed in warm water and soap after drying thoroughly. Acrylics provide a durable surface but should not be dry-cleaned. They seem to work best on materials made of natural fibers—cotton, linen, and wool.

Textile paints designed especially for fabrics usually work nicely. Follow the manufacturer's directions carefully. The paint seems to be thick enough to produce a clean-cut design. Textile paints can be used for all types of material, especially those that require dry cleaning.

Latex paints can also be used. However, the consistency is rather thin, which may allow bleeding. It is better to work with a fairly dry brush.

Procedures to Follow

Position the stencil carefully. Hold it in place with pins or tacks. It is most important that the stencil remain in place, adhering closely to the fabric. As you work, press down the edges with your free hand close to the area to which you are applying the paint. If the area is too narrow to hold down with your finger, use a pointed tool.

Using the Brush. Dip the tip of the brush into the paint. Remove any excess by dabbing it on brown paper. It is best to work with a fairly dry brush so the paint will not run under the edge of the stencil. Testing the application on a scrap of fabric will give you some idea as to how the paint reacts to the fabric. If it seems to bleed, you know the paint is too thin. Dab the brush several times until you are sure the reaction is just right.

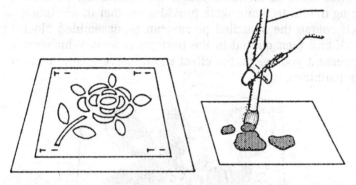

Hold the brush upright, perpendicular to the fabric and stencil. Use an up-and-down dabbing motion. Do not sweep the brush over the surface. Work along the outside edges first. Hold the edges of the stencil firmly in place. When this is completed fill in the center area. Sometimes it is necessary to apply more

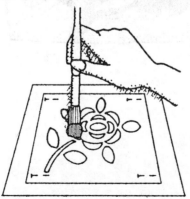

than one coat of paint to create the correct effect. Be sure the first coat is dry before applying the second.

Sometimes, when working on dark fabric, it seems best to stencil in white for a first layer and allow it to dry thoroughly before applying the color.

ADDED TOUCHES

Stenciling provides a nice background for quilting stitches. Using contour quilting around the design sets it off in a pleasing fashion. Padding the motif seems to enhance the effect. Combining it with trapunto work provides another interesting look.

Of course the stenciled pieces can be assembled block by block and then quilted in the traditional way. Whichever arrangement you select, the effect should have a certain charming quaintness.

14

Putting It All Together

Putting the blocks together, whether they have been appliquéd, pieced, or just quilted, is the next step in quilting. It can be done in various ways, depending on the effect you wish to create. The arrangement that is used is referred to as the "set."

The Set

Three basic ways of assembling the blocks are mentioned here. In some instances the procedure itself seems to frame them, providing a background so the decorative feature can be enjoyed more.

Adjacent Blocks. Although this is an easy way to sew the blocks together, it has the potential for producing a surprising number of looks. By turning the block, a different effect is created. The interaction of adjacent blocks produces looks that are not apparent in the single block. Setting the blocks verti-

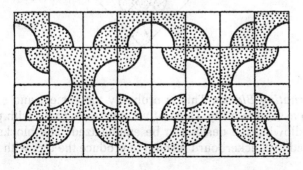

cally and horizontally will provide a design quite different than if they are arranged diagonally. Turning a block one quarter will often change the design in an amazing way.

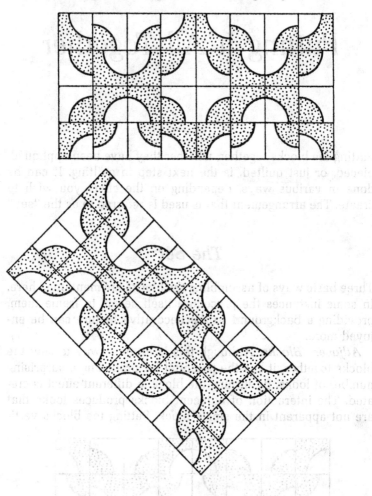

Alternating Blocks. This is probably the easiest and safest way to assemble a top. Decorative blocks alternate with plain ones, allowing the designs to be emphasized. The blocks are arranged in checkerboard fashion to produce the top, with each

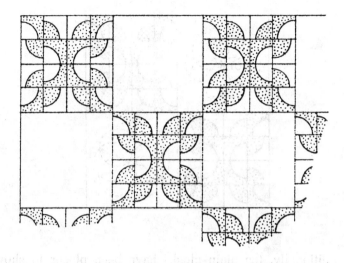

square keeping its original identity. The blocks can be arranged horizontally and vertically or, if you wish, diagonally. In case you decide to work in diagonal fashion, triangular sections will be needed to complete the top along the edges and corners.

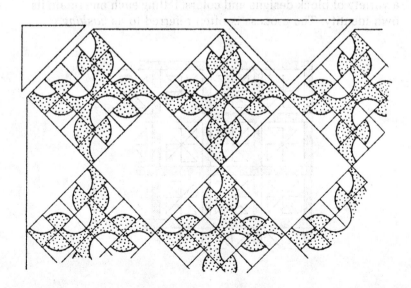

Traditionally, the plain blocks have been places to show beautiful workmanship. Intricate designs outlined in tiny stitches have been featured.

Lattice Strips. Strips of fabric are sometimes put between the blocks. When the dividers are sewn in place, they produce a lattice effect. The strips mark the boundaries of each block, giving an orderly look to the top. They seem to bring a unity to a variety of block designs and colors, letting each one retain its own identity. The process is often referred to as *sashing*.

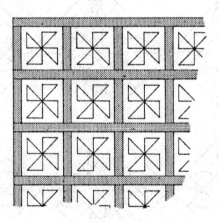

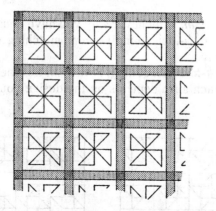

Narrow, rectangular strips of fabric are sewn between the blocks as well as between rows of blocks to complete the design. The strips can be made of plain or printed material and used as an unbroken band. If a more decorative effect is desired, the strips can be divided by squares at the intersections. Contrasting colors and patterned fabric add interest.

If you decide to set the blocks together with lattice following a diagonal direction, you will need two additional triangular pieces. Use a template to cut each. One will be one fourth the size of the intersection square; the other, one half.

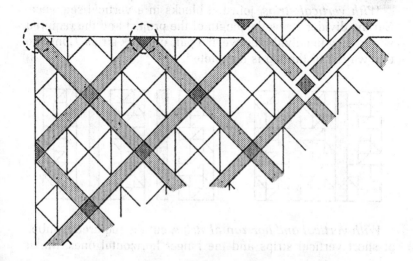

Sewing the Set. Whichever way you have decided to join the blocks, use a ¼-inch (6-mm) seam, matching crossing seam lines carefully.

For a block-to-block setting, sew them together in strips. The number in each strip depends on the design you have planned for the top.

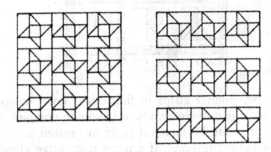

If you are working with patchwork blocks, press the seams to one side. Alternate the direction. For instance, on one strip press the seams to the left and on the next one to the right. With the strips of blocks made, join them together in the planned sequence. Again, match the crossing seam lines precisely. Press these seam allowances down.

With vertical strips, join the blocks in a vertical sequence. Cut the divider strips the length of the project and the required width. Sew the divider between a pair of block strips. Continue this way until the top is completed.

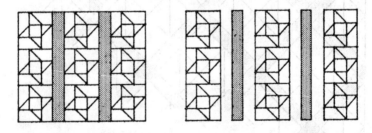

With vertical and horizontal strips, cut the required number of short vertical strips and the longer horizontal ones. Make horizontal strips using the blocks and vertical dividers, sewing a vertical divider between a pair of block strips.

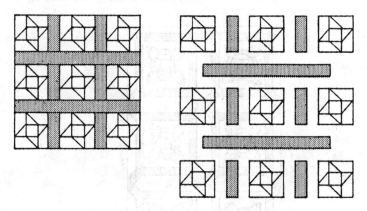

Then join the horizontal block strips with horizontal divider strips. One strip is placed between each pair of the block strips.

For a diagonal setting, the blocks are sewn together to form strips. These strips will then be arranged diagonally to form the top. The length of each strip will depend on its placement in the total design. Because the edge of the finished project must be straight, it is necessary to trim the strips so only a partial block remains. In joining the strips, work from the center to the outer edges in an alternating sequence.

For a decorative touch, bands of appliqué can be added to the divider strips. Cut them on the bias so they can be arranged in curving lines such as the design shown here. In planning the

design, the width of the strip should be given careful consideration. Keep it in proportion to the wider one.

Turn under the edges 1/4 inch (6 mm) and press. Pin the bands in the correct position and baste. Then sew them in place with tiny stitches.

The Border

A border can be the finishing touch. It frames the decorative design, defining its size and emphasizing its beauty. It should complement the central design. Although many quilted projects are made without borders, the use of one is a factor that should be considered carefully. A border seems to tie the designs together, bringing a certain unity as it confines an all-over design pattern so it doesn't seem to run off into space. It is important

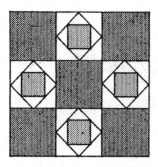 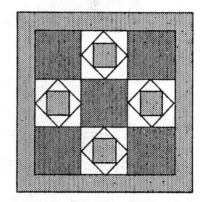

to remember that the border should accentuate the main design and not take attention away from it.

The border should be planned as part of the total design instead of as an afterthought. In this way it becomes an integral part of the entire pattern. It may continue to follow straight lines or be shaped to add a new dimension. The fabric can be of one color or patterned, left plain or embellished with stitches, piecing, or appliqué.

Width of Border. There are no rules to help you decide on the correct width. It depends on the look you want and on your artistic sense. A quilted piece might look equally well with either wide or narrow borders. For instance, a large quilt made up of many repetitive blocks may need a wide border for a definite change, whereas another pattern requiring space for building may look better with a narrow one. Of course the block size as well as the finished size of the project will influence your decision.

Color for Border. In Chapter 2 you will find some suggestions for working with color (see page 21). Deciding on the color scheme is most important. Generally, it is best to use the color or colors that are in the center design, following a principle for using color that results in a lovely, harmonious color plan. Introducing a new color is more difficult to do, although the effect may be interesting.

Quilting the Border. The solid or whole-cloth border is probably the one most often used. It not only provides a plain area for working a beautiful quilting design, but it also brings unity to the color scheme as it encloses the design area.

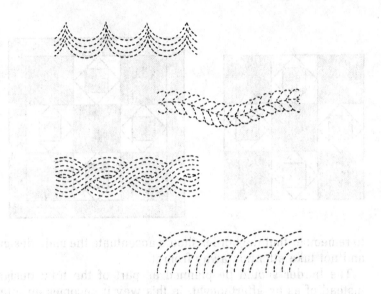

To have the proper impact, the border should reflect the mood of the main pattern. Almost any design that is appropriate for long, narrow areas can be employed. Traditional designs featured curving motifs moving in wavelike lines, such as swags, feathers, cables, interlocking circles or diamonds.

In planning the border design, be sure to mark the center point on each side. Starting at the corners, work toward the middle. At this point you should have completed one whole or one half of a repeat. If this doesn't happen, then adapt the design slightly until it fits correctly.

Turning the corners requires special attention. The design

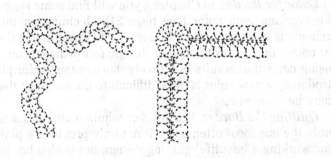

should flow smoothly around the area, giving a balanced look on both sides.

Sometimes a different motif is introduced in the corners. However, the design seems more pleasing if the motif is related to the basic border pattern. At times the pattern can be adapted to fit the corner, allowing the design to flow around it in a continuous line.

If the components of the design are definite, the complete border must be carefully planned so full repeats can be made.

This means that the length and width of the border should be calculated precisely. It will be easier to make your plans on graph paper. In this way, you can adjust the design measurements as well as the project measurements if this is necessary.

Pieced Border. This type of border can act as an extension of the main design or introduce a variation of it. Probably the

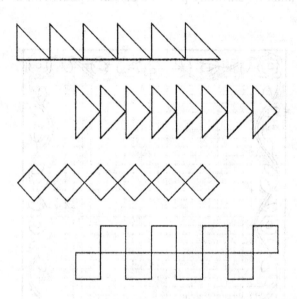

easiest way to create this type of design is to alter the block by changing the color or by adding or subtracting a pattern detail.

Simple bands of various shapes, such as triangles, squares, and diamonds, can be attractive. If the shapes repeat those in the block, the results are effective. Deciding on the corner design of the border and then adding straight pieces by extending the seam lines of the block offers another possibility.

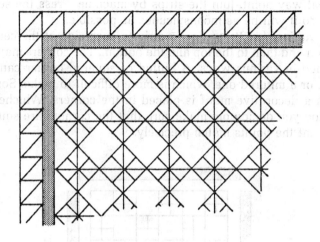

Sometimes the effect will be best if a plain strip is inserted between the central portion of the quilt and the border.

Preparing the Border. Measurements are important. Be sure to keep the dimensions of the article as you planned them. It is these original measurements that should be used to cut the border pieces, not those of the center area. As you quilt or piece, there is a tendency for the material to stretch, or to be gathered if the stitches are pulled too tightly. This can increase or decrease the outer dimensions of the decorative area, changing the desired size requirements. If the side of the top is shorter than it should be, stretch it slightly as it is sewed to the border. However, if it is too long, ease in the fullness as you sew.

Cutting the Strips. Cut the strips on the lengthwise grain. Measure the width from the selvage. If the selvage edge isn't straight, draw a straight line along the selvage to indicate the lengthwise thread. Then measure from this line. Remember to allow for the seam allowances.

Cut each strip the required length. If you wish to use less fabric, you may decide to piece the strip. This can be done at the halfway point. Join the strips by machine. Press the seam open so it will be as inconspicuous as possible.

Attaching the Strips. Sew a strip to each side of the center section and then to the top and the bottom. The corners may be finished in various ways. A butted or squared corner can be used, or a mitered one, which is more difficult to make. Sometimes a decorative motif is placed in the corners. Whichever method you decide on, make sure that the corners are square and that the points match precisely.

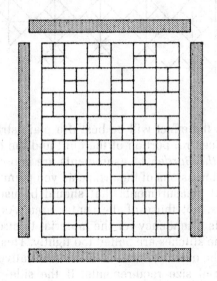

15

Easy Quilting Projects

Although quilting is most often thought of in connection with quilts, it does have other possibilities. Browsing through a department store makes one realize how often quilting is added to various articles. A pot holder for the kitchen, a hanger for the closet, a place mat for the dining room, a pillow for the sofa, and a pocket for a jacket are some of the places you may find a quilted motif. Recently a well-known clothes designer used quilting to add distinctive touches to his collection: a rolling collar, a patch pocket, and a bolero featuring quilting, with each looking new and attractive.

Many of the items offer excellent suggestions for beginning projects. Testing your quilting ability on something small is always a good idea. Transforming a practice piece into a pretty, useful article takes the drudgery out of practice.

If you sew, you know how handy it is to have your own basic pattern. For quilting, the basic pattern is very often just a geometric shape. Squares, rectangles, and circles are frequently used. Employed flat or folded, they can be converted into a number of interesting articles.

Quilting Your Own Fabric

A good way to start your quilting experience is simply to quilt a piece of material with a sewing machine. Then use it to make a variety of items. This allows you to proceed, when you are using a commercial pattern, as if you had purchased quilted material by the yard.

PREPARE LAYERS

After selecting appropriate fabrics, arrange the three layers in the correct fashion. Baste them together carefully, beginning in the center and progressing toward the sides. Diagonal basting works well. Rolling the material as it passes under the arm of the machine makes it easier to control the work. Be sure that the tension, pressure, and stitch length are correctly adjusted so that you do not stitch tiny pleats into the fabric.

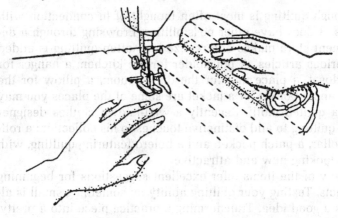

AMOUNT TO QUILT

The type and amount of fabric you quilt will depend on what you plan to make. For instance, if you quilted 1 yard of 45-inch fabric, you could make 10 pot holders or the tops for 6 place mats. If you are in the mood to be thrifty, this is an excellent way to express it. Not only are you saving money but also you are using your creative ability at the same time. Watch for a sale of designer sheets. From a twin sheet you can make 8 place mats, 8 napkins, and a runner for the center of your table. Just think how much money you will be saving and still have something that is distinctively your own.

Articles to Make

To help you with this endeavor, some quick and easy projects are suggested here. They can be made without commercial patterns. All you need to have are some measurements and general directions for making each one. You can supply the creativity to produce an attractive item using a basic shape.

FROM A SQUARE PIECE OF FABRIC

It is amazing how many different things you can make using a square as the basic pattern. Small and large alike, the shape lends itself nicely to quilting projects.

Pot Holder. A pot holder may not seem to be a very exciting item on which to begin your quilting experience, but it does offer many opportunities to try out some of your imaginative

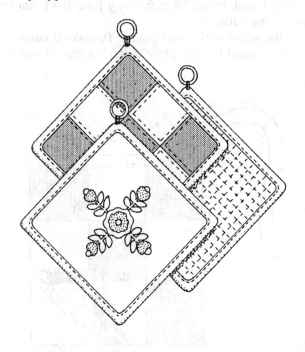

ideas. Start with a basic square. One about 7 inches (18 cm) plus seam allowances seems a handy size to use.

You can make the pot holder from scraps of appropriate fabric or from 1/4 yard (23 cm) of new material. Of course, if you are combining colors, you will need yardage in each color. In some stores that have quilting supplies, you may be able to buy fabric in small pieces. You will also need batting, thread, double-fold bias binding, and a plastic ring.

For an all-over design of stitches, place the stitching lines about 1 inch (2.5 cm) apart. Use them vertically, horizontally, or diagonally, combining them if you wish. The checks or diamonds that evolve form the pattern.

For patchwork, you might try the popular nine-patch. Using pieces 3 inches (8 cm) square will produce a pot holder about 8 inches (20.5 cm) square. Join the pieces with 1/4-inch (6-mm) seams. After assembling the layers, use matching thread to quilt around each piece, 1/4 inch away from the seam line except along the outer edges.

Finish the edges with bias binding. To make it easier to bind the corners, round them slightly. Attach a ring at one corner.

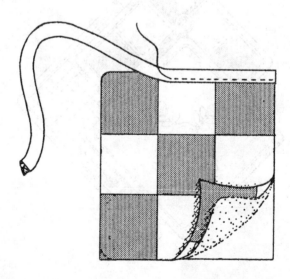

Hot Pad. A pieced hot pad can add a colorful touch to an informal table setting. For added interest, you might tuck a bit of potpourri inside. The warmth of a steaming teapot or a sizzling casserole will produce the proper conditions for releasing a pleasing aroma.

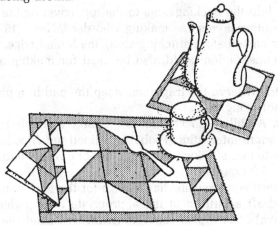

A square of patchwork or crazy quilting of your preferred design can be used. As for size, an 8-inch (20-cm) one works nicely.

To make the pad you will need sufficient scraps to make the top layer, a 10¼-inch (25.5-cm) square for the backing, enough batting to make two 8-inch (20-cm) squares, and ½ ounce of potpourri of your choice.

After completing the decorative square, press all edges of the backing piece to the wrong side ¼ inch (6 mm). Lay it on a flat

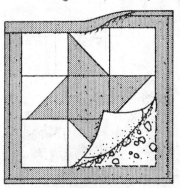

surface with the wrong side up. On it, center a square of batting. Sprinkle the potpourri evenly over the batting. Add the second square of batting, covering the potpourri. Finally put the decorative square on top of the layers with the right side up.

Carefully fold the backing edge to the top, covering the raw edges of the other layers and making a border 5/8 inch (15 mm) wide. Pin or baste before stitching along the folded edge. This method of construction could also be used for making a pot holder.

In order to preserve the fragrance, keep the pad in a plastic bag when not being used.

A Pocket. A quilted pocket can often make a simple jacket seem much more interesting. Probably a lined patch pocket is the best one to use, although you could use one with a flap. Just the flap could be quilted.

If the pattern you are using has a piece for the pocket, use it. Otherwise draft a pattern in the appropriate size, perhaps 6 inches (15 cm) square plus seam allowances. Round the two lower corners slightly.

Plan the design to fit the mood of the costume you are making. A series of vertical lines works nicely for a collar and pocket combination. Also a double row of stitches placed

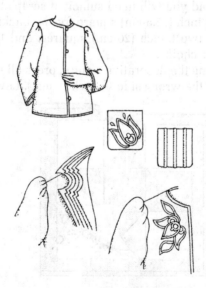

about 1/4 inch (6 mm) apart with the double rows put about 3/4 inch (2 cm) apart can make an attractive pattern. For a dressy outfit, curved lines create a more elaborate look. A small scroll, flower, or feather may produce the right effect.

Using appropriate fabric that is light or medium in weight, cut out the pocket. For the backing, use a sheer fabric; for the inner layer, batting.

After decorating the pocket, sew the lining piece to the pocket with right sides together, leaving a section of lower edge open for turning. The lining piece should be cut the same size as the pocket and of matching fabric. The jacket fabric can be used, unless it makes the pocket seem too bulky, or a color-matched lining material.

After seaming, trim and grade the seam. Cut across corners and notch curved areas in order to remove excess fabric in the seam allowance. Work gently as you pass the pocket through the opening at the lower edge. Adjust the corners and roll the seam to the back so it will not be seen on the right side. Press pocket lightly. Close the opening by slip stitching the folded edges together. Pin the pocket into its proper position and slip stitch in place.

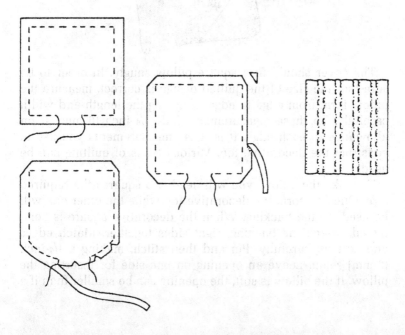

For another look, you might combine the pockets with a quilted roll collar. It will add a luxurious effect to a robe or evening jacket when a fabric such as satin is being used.

A Pillow. Pillows offer an ideal way to use patchwork samples. They are quick and easy to make and at the same time provide a decorative touch to various décors. A knife-edge pillow works well. Cording or a novelty trim can be added, although the plain seaming seems appropriate.

The cover should fit a square pillow snugly. In order to be sure that the size of the quilted design is correct, measure the pillow form from edge to edge, checking the length and width carefully. To these measurements, add 1/4 inch (6 mm) seam allowance to each edge. It is these measurements you use to construct the decorative top. Various types of quilting can be used.

To make the pillow, you will need two squares the required size. One will form the decorative top while the other one will be used for the backing. When the decorative square is completed, attach the backing, right sides together. Match edges and corners carefully. Pin and then stitch, making a 1/4-inch (6-mm) seam. Leave an opening on one side for inserting the pillow. If the pillow is soft, the opening can be smaller than if a

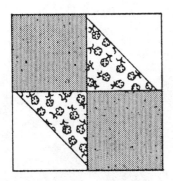 

firm one is being used. Press along the seam lines. Cut across the corners so they remain sharp when cover is turned.

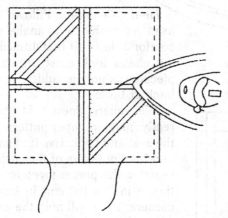

Turn cover inside out. Insert pillow. Be sure the case fits the corners squarely. Fold in seam allowances on both sides of the opening. Slip stitch the folded edges together, closing the opening. Smooth out the top so there are no wrinkles.

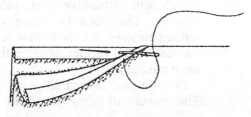

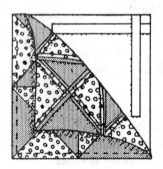

Tie-on Cushions. Pillows can also be used as cushions to make chairs more comfortable to sit in. Old-fashioned rocking chairs look most attractive when a pieced cushion is added to the seat or back or both.

If a square doesn't fit the chair correctly, make a paper pattern the shape of the seat and back. Use it to cut out the top and bottom layers of the cushions. Before seaming the pieces together, insert fabric ties, 8 inches (20 cm) in length, at back corners. They will hold the cushion in position. Remember, just one end of each strip should be stitched in place. Complete the cushion as you did the pillow.

Tote Bag. It is possible to make a functional and attractive bag using two squares. They can be made of plain quilted material or a decorative one, using any one of the various patterns that have been mentioned.

Prepare two 15-inch (37.5-cm) squares. The amount of fabric you need will depend on the design you are using. If you are working with batting, cut away the seam allowances so the batting will not be caught in the stitching as the two squares are seamed together.

Pin the two squares together, right sides facing. Stitch a 1/4-inch (6-mm) seam along the lower edge.

To produce a boxed effect, turn up each lower corner 2 inches (5 cm), inserting the raw edges between the side seams. Pin and then stitch a 1/4-inch (6-mm) seam. You will be stitching through four thicknesses of fabric for about 2 inches (5 cm). When you turn the bag to the right side, folded triangles will appear at each corner.

For a better seam finish, cover the raw edges with a folded bias binding. It can be sewn in place by hand if the thickness of the layers is too bulky.

For the handles, use webbing, 1 inch (2.5 cm) wide, in a matching or contrasting color. Cut two strips, 22 inches (55 cm) long. Pin one strip to the right side of the front and to the back, 3 1/2 inches (8.5 cm) in from the side seams.

To finish the top of the bag, cut a strip of matching fabric 2 inches (5 cm) wide and 29 inches (72.5 cm) long for a facing. Fold under one short edge 1/2 inch (1.2

cm). Pin strip to top of bag, right sides together, with the handles between the bag and the facing. Stitch 1/2 inch (1.2 cm) from the edge. Press along the stitching line. Turn the facing to the wrong side. Baste it in place so the seam line is along the edge. Edge-stitch 1/8 inch (3 mm) from folded edge. Turn under the raw edge of the facing 1/2 inch (1.2 cm). Pin in place and stitch. Slip stitch the folded end in place.

USING A RECTANGLE

Although the rectangular shape is not as convenient to use for patchwork as the square, it does work nicely as a basic pattern for other types of quilting. Place mats, and cases for lingerie and eyeglasses are just a few of the items you can make with a rectangle.

Place Mats. Place mats are quick and easy to make. They can be decorated in innumerable ways. Quilting the fabric by machine, using one of the geometric designs, is most effective, especially when it is used on a patterned fabric. In planning the design, always consider the effect when the china, silver, and glassware are in place.

Begin by preparing the quilted material in any way that seems appropriate and effective. For four place mats, you will need 3/4 yard (0.70 m) of 45-inch (115 cm) quilted material. There will be a few extra inches that you can use for coasters or a narrow runner for the center of the table. Crossing diagonal lines or a zigzag pattern produce an interesting effect.

Cut a pattern 17 inches (42.5 cm) by 12 inches (30 cm). Use it to cut out the place mat, being careful to keep the edges on the grain line. If there is a definite design pattern to the fabric, center it so the finished place mat looks attractive. Gently round the corners. This makes it easier to bind the edges.

To bind the edges, use a bias binding at least 7/8 inch (22 mm) wide. You can use a commercial bias tape or cut the binding from matching or contrasting fabric.

Apply the binding by hand or machine, depending on the effect you want. Begin on a side, not at a corner. Remember, one end of the bias must be turned under. Which one will depend on how you are applying the bias. If you are encasing the edge, then the finishing end will be turned under 1/4 inch

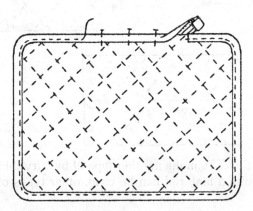

(6 mm); but if you are sewing the bias first to one side and then the other, the beginning end should be folded under. Pin and sew the bias in place.

Bag or Case. Believe it or not, a place mat can be folded, transforming it into a clutch bag or a glove case. Of course, the type of material the place mat is made of will influence the way it is used.

To make the bag, just turn up one end 6½ inches (16.2 cm), leaving a 4-inch (10-cm) flap. Stitch the ends together. Add a snap and you have a flat bag.

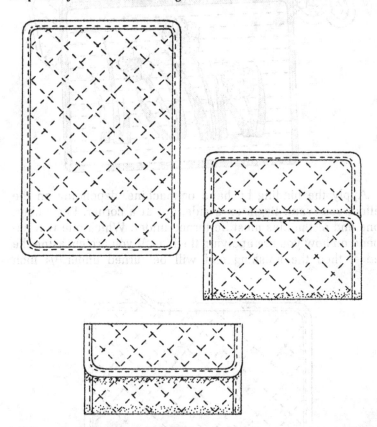

Lingerie Case. To make another type of bag, try this method. Although quilted material can be used, other types of quilting are most appropriate. They will give you a chance to test your ability to make tiny quilting stitches as well as doing trapunto, appliqué, and embroidery. Adding a dainty touch to the flap seems just right.

The cases can be made in a variety of sizes. You may even want to make a set of cases. They are especially handy to have when traveling. Such items as slips and panty hose can each have a case, keeping your suitcase in order and easy to pack. After deciding what type of quilting you are going to use, cut a rectangle in the proper size.

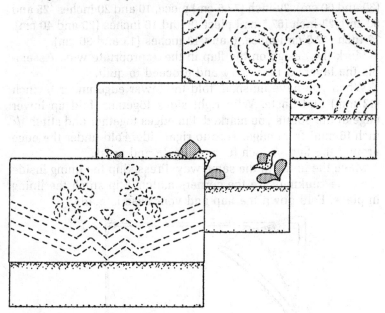

For a case about 10 by 6 inches (25 by 15 cms) with a 5-inch (12.5-cm) flap, cut a rectangle 17 by 6 inches (42.5 by 15 cm).

For a case about 12 by 8 inches (30 by 20 cm) with a 7-inch (17.5-cm) flap, cut a rectangle 23 by 8 inches (57.5 by 20 cm).

For a case about 14 by 10 inches (35 by 25 cm) with a 9-inch (22.5-cm) flap, cut a rectangle 29 by 10 inches (72.5 by 25 cm).

For a case 16 by 12 inches (40 by 30 cm) with an 11-inch (27.5-cm) flap, cut a rectangle 35 by 12 inches (87.5 by 30 cm).

You will need fabric for the outside or top layer as well as the lining. Use lightweight fabrics. They can be of luxurious silk or a more serviceable cotton. It just depends on how you are going to use them. A yard (90 cm) of 45-inch (115 cm) material and another yard for the lining will allow you to make the four cases. In order to create the quilted effect you will need batting as well as some sheer material for the backing.

After cutting out the rectangles, mark the seam allowances on both sides to indicate where the folds should be placed. On the 35-inch (87.5-cm) piece, place the marks at 12 and 24 inches (30 and 60 cm); 29-inch (72.5-cm) piece, 10 and 20 inches (25 and 50 cm); 23-inch (57.5-cm) piece, 8 and 16 inches (20 and 40 cm); 17-inch (42.5 cm) piece, 6 and 12 inches (15 and 30 cm).

Mark the design on the flap in the appropriate way. Assemble the layers if necessary and proceed to quilt.

When you have finished, fold the lower edge under 1/2 inch (12 mm) and baste. With right sides together, fold up lower edge at the points you marked. Pin edges together and stitch 1/4 inch (6 mm) from edge. Turn to right side. Fold under the edge around the flap 1/4 inch (6 mm). Baste and press.

Make the lining in the same way. Press. Slip the lining inside the case, making sure the corners match. Slip stitch the lining in place. Fold down the flap and your case is made.

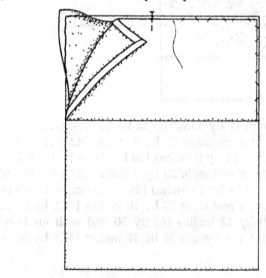

Eyeglass Case. Quilted fabric offers a good padded protection for glasses and does it in an attractive way. The decorative motif can vary according to your personal preferences. Colorful crazy quilting or good-looking trapunto works equally well.

For a case measuring approximately 6½ by 3¼ inches (16.5 by 8.3 cm), you will need a set of rectangles 5 by 14 inches (12.5 by 35 cm). One rectangle will be the outside fabric, which is the top layer. Then there is a rectangle for batting and backing fabric, and finally the lining.

After cutting the rectangles from the quilted material, fold them in half crosswise, making sure that the raw edges match exactly. Pin and stitch ½ inch (1.3 cm) from the edges. Trim seams and corners. Turn to right side.

Make lining in the same way. Press. Insert the case with wrong sides together. Match seams and raw edges. Baste raw edges together. Finish these edges with bias binding cut from a matching fabric.

USING A CIRCLE

This shape does not seem to offer as many quilting possibilities as the square and the rectangle. Of course such items as pot holders, place mats, and bags can be done in circular form. One article that seems to look especially attractive is the round table cover. The flare of the curving edge is most pleasing.

Round Table Cover. The cover is cut from quilted material and then finished in various ways, depending on the look you want. A binding, a facing, or a turned and stitched edge can be used. Even a bit of trimming can be added if desired.

To determine the size of the circle, some measurements must be taken. You need to know the diameter of the circle. To ob-

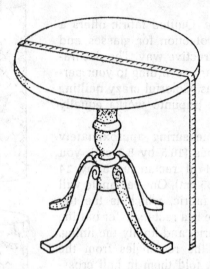

tain this measurement, take the height of the table, times two, plus the diameter of the table. If you do not want to make the cover extend to the floor, the measurement for height will be less. You can adjust the size to meet your needs.

To make a pattern for a circle, take a square of paper the correct size and fold it in half. Then fold it in half again. With a tape measure or yardstick and pencil, mark the outline of the circle. Using one half of the diameter measurement, measure from the point along the folded edges. Continue to mark, always pivoting from the point, making an arc. Be sure to measure accurately. When you have finished, cut out the circle along the markings.

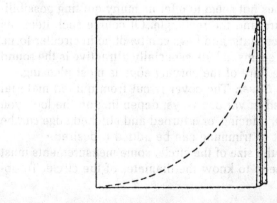

Pin the pattern to the quilted material and cut out the circle. Finish the edges in an appropriate fashion.

A Quilt from a Square, Rectangle, or Circle

We don't often think of a quilt as being a square or rectangle, but it really is. It can even be a circle in shape. Just as smaller projects can be made using the basic shapes, so can a quilt. Some general directions will make this undertaking easier to do.

MEASURING

Before starting a quilt, it is necessary to take some measurements. By deciding where and how you will use the quilt, you can plan the design to fit the space properly and can determine the size it should be.

If it is to be used on a bed, begin by measuring the bed, which should be fully made with sheets, blankets, and pillows in place. Without them the measurements would be shorter. Using a flexible tape measure is thought to provide the most accurate measurements.

Measure the top length and width of the bed and the depth from the top of the mattress to the floor. Also measure the depth of the mattress and from the top of the box spring to the floor.

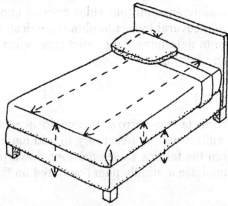

For a bedspread, the quilt should fall to the floor and cover the pillows. This means that it must be made longer to allow for a tuck-in under the pillows. Usually about 15 inches (37.5 cm) is allowed. To determine the needed measurements, remember to add the depth of both sides to the basic width measurement and the depth at the end and tuck-in to the length.

For a coverlet, the quilt will be smaller. It should be made to cover the top mattress and overlap the box spring by about 2 or 3 inches (5 or 7.5 cm). A separate dust ruffle covers the box spring.

To determine the length of the coverlet, add the depth of the mattress plus 2 or 3 inches (5 or 7.5 cm) to the top length plus the tuck-in allowance if the quilt is to cover the pillows. For the width, add the depth of the mattress and 2 or 3 inches (5 or 7.5 cm) on each side for the overlap to the top width.

CUTTING SIZE

Although the measurements you have just taken are most important, there are other factors to be considered in planning the size. There is a tendency for the materials to draw together as they are quilted. This type of shrinkage can cause a quilt to become 3 to 6 inches (7.5 to 15 cm) smaller. The amount of shrinkage seems to depend on the thickness of the batting and the amount of quilting. The thicker the batting and the more quilting, the greater the reduction in size. It may be wise to make a test piece before determining the cutting size.

The edge finish will also influence the size. A 1/2-inch (1.2-cm) seam allowance on four sides may be enough, or you may have to add several inches to obtain the desired measurements. Be sure to determine the correct size before cutting out the backing and batting.

ADDED WIDTH

When a fabric is too narrow to extend across the entire width of the quilt it will be necessary to add material to each side. Never join the fabrics so a seam runs down the center of the quilt. Instead use a middle panel centered on the top of the

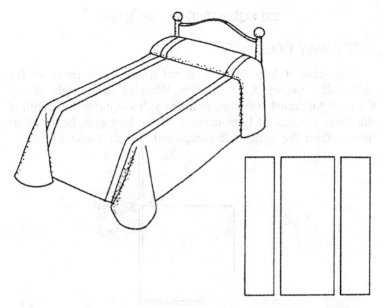

bed with matching panels added to each side. If necessary, a border of the appropriate width can be added to increase the size of the quilt.

ROUNDING A CORNER

A curve at the corner produces a nice finish. To mark the quilt with a curving line, work on the wrong side. Draw a square at the corners of the foot end equal to the depth of the drop. Marking as you did for the round table cover (see page 264), measure from the inner corner, creating a curving line. Baste on this line, transferring the curved line to the right side. Repeat this procedure on the opposite corner. After the quilt is completed, cut on the marked line.

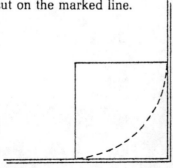

CUT AWAY CORNERS

Sometimes it is necessary to cut away the corners so the quilt will fit around the foot posts. Working on the right side of the quilt top, mark a square with the sides equal to the depth of the drop. Do this at both corners of the foot end. Baste along lines. When the quilting is completed, cut on marked lines.

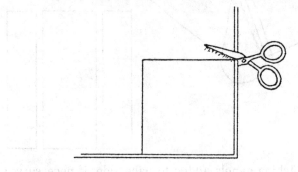

Bibliography

When preparing a manuscript, I always browse through many books on the subject. They stimulate my thinking and provide interesting background material. Some of the books and booklets I found most informative are mentioned here. I think you will enjoy them also.

Avery, Virginia. *Quilts to Wear*. Charles Scribner's Sons, 1983.

Better Homes and Gardens, Editors. *American Patchwork and Quilting*. Meredith Corporation, 1985.

Bishop, Robert, and Elizabeth Safanda. *A Gallery of Amish Quilts*. E. P. Dutton, Inc., 1976.

Bonesteel, Georgia. *Lap Quilting*. Oxmoor House, Inc., 1982.

Echols, Margit. *The Quilter's Start-to-Finish Workbook*. Barnes & Noble Books, 1979.

Fairfield, Helen. *Patchwork*. Octopus Books Limited, 1980.

Fisher, Katharine, and Elizabeth Kay. *Quilting in Squares*. Charles Scribner's Sons, 1978.

Frager, Dorothy. *The Book of Sampler Quilts*. Chilton Book Company, 1983.

Guild, Vera P. *Good Housekeeping Book of Quilt Making*. Hearst Books, 1976.

Haywood, Dixie. *Crazy Quilt*. Crown Publishers, Inc., 1977.

Hinson, Dolores. *American Graphic Quilt Designs*. Arco Publishing, Inc., 1982.

Ickis, Marguerite. *Standard Book of Quilt Making and Collecting*. Dover Publications, Inc., 1949.

Jackson, Val, ed. *Beautiful Patchwork and Quilting Book*. Sterling Publishing Company, Inc., 1985.

James, Michael. *The Quiltmaker's Handbook*. Prentice-Hall, Inc., 1978.

————. *The Second Quiltmaker's Handbook*. Prentice-Hall, Inc., 1981.

Johnson, Mary Elizabeth. *A Garden of Quilts*. Oxmoor House, Inc., 1984.

Johnston, Susan. *Early American Patchwork Quilts to Color*. Dover Publications, Inc., 1984.

Larsen, Judith La Belle, and Carol Waugh Gull. *The Patchwork Quilt Design and Coloring Book*. New Century Publishers, Inc., 1977.

McCall's Needlework and Crafts Publication Editors. *Antique Quilts*. The McCall Pattern Company, 1974.

————. *Heirloom Quilts*. The McCall Pattern Company.

————. *Quilt It*. The McCall Pattern Company, 1973.

McCall's Sewing Book. Random House/McCall's, 1968.

Malone, Maggie. *120 Patterns for Traditional Patchwork Quilts*. Sterling Publishing Company, Inc., 1983.

————. *115 Classic American Patchwork Quilt Patterns*. Sterling Publishing Company, Inc., 1984.

Martin, Judy. *Patchwork Book*. Charles Scribner's Sons, 1983.

Mills, Susan Winter. *Illustrated Index to Traditional American Quilt Patterns*. Arco Publishing, Inc., 1981.

Nelson, Cyril I, and Carter Houck. *The Quilt Engagement Calendar Treasury*. E. P. Dutton, Inc., 1982.

Morris Museum of Arts and Sciences, Curator of Decorative Arts. *New Jersey Quilter*.

Ondori Publishing Co. Staff. *Patchwork and Quilting Book*. Ondorisha Publishers, Ltd., 1981.

Pyman, Kit, ed. *Every Kind of Patchwork*. Chartwell Books, Inc., 1983.

Quilt National. *The Quilt: New Directions for an American Tradition*. Schiffer Publishing, Ltd., 1983.

Plenary Publications International, Inc. Editors. *The Family Creative Workshop*, Vol. 14. Plenary Publications International, Inc., 1975.

Reader's Digest Editors. *Complete Guide to Needlework.* The Reader's Digest Association, Inc., 1979.

———. *Crafts and Hobbies.* The Reader's Digest Association, Inc., 1979.

Risinger, Hettie. *Innovative Machine Patchwork Piecing.* Sterling Publishing Company, Inc., 1983.

Rogers, Josephine. *The 7-Day Quilt.* Van Nostrand Reinhold Company, Inc., 1979.

Safford, Carleton L., and Robert Bishop. *America's Quilts and Coverlets.* E. P. Dutton, Inc., 1980.

Singer Reference Library. *Sewing Essentials.* DeCosse Inc., 1984.

Strobl-Wohlschläger, Ilse. *Fun with Appliqué and Patchwork.* Watson-Guptill Publications, 1969.

Sunset Editors. *Quilting: Patchwork and Appliqué.* Lane Publishing Company, 1982.

Wilson, Erica. *Erica Wilson's Quilts of America.* Oxmoor House, Inc., 1979.

Sources
for Quilting Supplies

If, by any chance, you find it difficult to locate appropriate fabrics and equipment in your locality, you may want to contact one of the mail-order companies listed here. Some will provide you with a catalog free or for a small charge. The type and variety of supplies offered by each company will vary.

Come Quilt With Me, Box 1063, Brooklyn, New York, 11202–1063.

Contemporary Quilts, 5305 Denwood Avenue, Memphis, Tennessee, 38119.

Country House Quilt, 170 South Main Street, Zionsville, Indiana, 46077.

Country Quilt Shop, Box 91-D, Uniontown, Maryland 21157.

The Crafter's Gallery, Box 1400, Tenafly, New Jersey, 07670.

Cross Patch Quilting Center, Route 9, Garrison, New York, 10524.

The Hand Maiden, 1521 Ridgeway Road, Dayton, Ohio, 45419.

Hearthside Quilts, RD 2, Route 7, Shelburne, Vermont, 05482.

Herrschner's Inc., Hoover Road, Stevens Point, Wisconsin, 54481.

Home-Sew, Bethlehem, Pennsylvania, 18018.

Marge Murphy's, P. O. Box 6306, 6624 April Bayou, Biloxi, Mississippi, 39532.

Newark Dressmaker Supply Inc., 6473 Ruch Road, Box 2448, Lehigh Valley, Pennsylvania, 18001.

Pangle's Fabrics and Craft Center, Inc., 138 East Main Street, Wise, Virginia, 24293.

Patches and Patchwork, 216 Main Street, Portland, Connecticut, 06480.

Quilt Markings, P. O. Box 8163, Wichita, Kansas, 67208.

Quilters' Peace, P. O. Box 349, Garrison, New York, 10524.

Quilts and Other Comforts, Box 390, 6700 West 44th Avenue, Wheatridge, Colorado, 80034–0394.

Scarborough Flair, 4442 N.E. 131st Place, Portland, Oregon, 97230.

Seminole Sampler, P. O. Box 658, Ellicott City, Maryland, 21043.

The Stearns Technical Textiles Company, 100 Williams Street, Cincinnati, Ohio, 45215.

Stencils and Stuff, 72 Twelfth Street N.W., Strasburg, Ohio, 44680.

The Strawberry Patch Calico Shop, RD 3, Box 44, Columbia Cross Roads, Pennsylvania, 16914.

T.J.'s Quick Quilter, 514 Fairway Drive, Kerrville, Texas, 78028.

Index

appliqué of divider strips,
240
block-to-block, 238
diagonal, 239
lattice strips, 236–37
with vertical and
horizontal strips, 238–39
with vertical strips, 238
Bodkins
for corded quilting, 134
definition of, 32
Bonded batting, 56, 204
Borders
attaching the strips, 246
butted borders, 32, *33*
choice of, 240–41
colors for, 241
corners of, 242–44
cutting the strips, 245–46
definition of, 35
for Hawaiian-style
appliqué, 155–56
hoop, quilting with, 112,
113
pieced borders, 244–45
preparation of, 245
quilting designs for, 102–4,
241–42
width of, 241
Bride's quilts
description of, 32
history of, 5
Brushes for stenciling, 229
Bunching, definition of, 32
Butted borders, *33*
definition of, 32
Buttonhole stitch, 69–70

C

Cardboard, 52–53
Cases, directions for quilting,
260–63
Catch stitch, 76
Cathedral Windows, 208–9
color and size, variations
in, 209
construction of, 210–14
materials for, 209
tools for, 209
Cavaliers, 7
Chain stitch, 70–72
Channel quilting, 134
Charted designs, 226–27
Chiaroscuro, definition of, 33
Circles
folding of, 164
pattern for, 264–65
Clip, definition of, 33
Clipping
of appliqué, 147
of corners, 89–90
Clothing, quilted, 1
collars, 252–54
history of, 3
jackets, 17, 19
pockets, 252–54
Collars, quilted, 252–54
Color harmony, 22–24
Color interest, 21
Colors
balance of, 18–19
of borders, 241
in combination, 22–24
in contemporary quilting,
8–9
dominant note, 15